BUTTERFLIES OF I

The WWF-OUP Nature Guides are simple and informative books on our natural environment.

Other books in the series
Trees of India
Fishes of India
Seashore Life of India

WWF-India is one of the largest non-governmental organizations in the country working for the conservation of bio-diversity and natural habitats. With a large programme base in species, forests, freshwater habitats, climate change, eco systems, livelihoods, and environment education and policy, WWF-India engages with multiple stakeholders—local communities, teachers and students, state and central governments, industry and civil society organizations—to ensure a living planet for future generations.
For more information, please visit www.wwfindia.org

BUTTERFLIES OF INDIA

THOMAS GAY
ISAAC DAVID KEHIMKAR
JAGDISH CHANDRA PUNETHA

Photographs by
ISAAC DAVID KEHIMKAR

WWF for a living planet®

OXFORD
UNIVERSITY PRESS

YMCA Library Building, Jai Singh Road, New Delhi 110 001

Oxford University Press is a department of the University of Oxford.
It furthers the University's objective of excellence in research, scholarship,
and education by publishing worldwide in

Oxford New York
Auckland Cape Town Dar es Salaam Hong Kong Karachi
Kuala Lumpur Madrid Melbourne Mexico City Nairobi
New Delhi Shanghai Taipei Toronto

With offices in
Argentina Austria Brazil Chile Czech Republic France Greece
Guatemala Hungary Italy Japan Poland Portugal Singapore
South Korea Switzerland Thailand Turkey Ukraine Vietnam

Oxford is a registered trade mark of Oxford University Press
in the UK and in certain other countries.

Published in India by
Oxford University Press, New Delhi

First published 2008
Second impression 2008

ISBN-13: 978-0-19-568801-6
ISBN-10: 0-19-568801-5

Typeset in Aldine401 BT
by Pealidezine, Vasant Kunj, Delhi 110 017
Printed in India at Thomson Press (India) Ltd, New Delhi-110 020
Published by Oxford University Press
YMCA Library Building, Jai Singh Road, New Delhi 110 001

CONTENTS

PREFACE

This book has been written for people who enjoy the beauty of butterflies and want to know more about them. There is, at present, no concise and non-specialist book on Indian butterflies, and perhaps this book will fill the gap to some extent.

Many butterflies have been killed for cabinet collections. It is now time to study living butterflies and enjoy their loveliness as they gambol in gardens or forests. The butterflies illustrated in this book have been photographed in their natural surroundings with all the ethics of wildlife photography being observed. None of the butterflies were killed, frozen, or struck for the sake of getting a perfect picture. Some of the species were reared and released in the wild after being photographed. Some butterflies do not normally rest with their wings open, so the upperside of their wings is rarely seen. In this book, the butterflies are shown in their most likely resting and basking position, which will facilitate their identification in the field. While some butterflies allow for close approach, others are extremely wary of 'strangers'. Thus, the butterflies here cannot be shown to scale. Their actual size (that is, wingspan—the distance from one wing tip to the other) is given in the text.

As far as possible, the language has been kept simple and non-technical. Technical words that could not be avoided have been explained in the glossary. Facts have been stated in broad outline, with details given in some cases of special interest. Such details may encourage some readers to study the subject more deeply. All that this book hopes to do is to open the door into the wonderland of butterflies and invite you to enter it. It is for each one of you to decide how far you wish to go.

INTRODUCTION

There are about 1500 species of butterflies in India. They vary greatly in colour, habits, and size. The largest butterfly, the Southern Birdwing (*Troides minos*), has a wingspan of up to 190 mm, while the smallest, the Grass Jewel (*Freyeria trochilus*), has a wingspan of 15 mm. The heroes and heroines of our book are some of the most common butterflies of India. Most of the features discussed in this book are shared with other butterflies in their respective groups, found in India as well as elsewhere.

Crab (Crustacea)

WHAT IS A BUTTERFLY?

A butterfly is a winged insect belonging to the phylum Arthropoda. In the animal kingdom, the Arthropoda group mainly includes creatures that have jointed limbs and a hard exoskeleton (In Greek, *arthros* means joined and *podos* means foot). The phylum is divided into five major classes: (1) Crustacea (crabs, lobsters, shrimps, etc.); (2) Myriapoda (centipedes and millipedes); (3) Insecta (silverfish, springtails, grasshoppers, butterflies, moths, etc.); (4) Arachnida (spiders, scorpions, ticks, etc.); and (5) Onychophora, which are considered a connecting link between Annelids (earthworms and leeches) and Arthropods. Insects form the largest class not only among the arthropods, but in the entire animal kingdom.

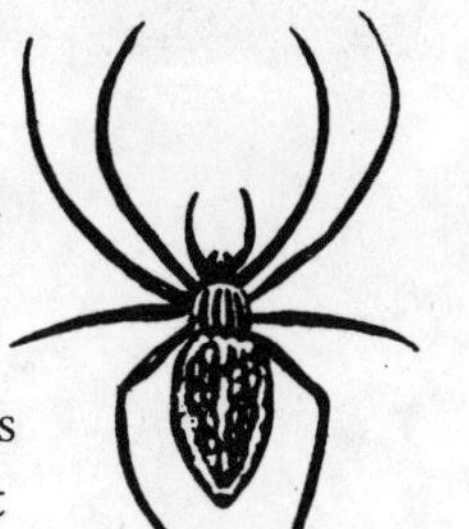

Spider (Arachnida)

Insects are further divided into twenty-nine orders that can be broadly grouped into winged (butterflies, moths, grasshoppers, etc.) and wingless (silver fish) insects. In fact, insects are the only invertebrates that can fly.

Butterflies belong to the order Lepidoptera, which means 'scale wings' (In Greek, *lepis* means scale and *pteron* means wing). The wings of butterflies are covered with tiny scales arranged like roof-tiles. These can all too easily be rubbed off as you will find if you hold a butterfly's wings between your fingers.

Centipede (Myriapoda)

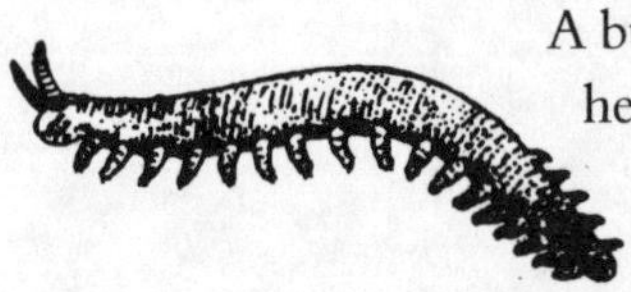

Peripaetus (Onychophora)

A butterflies, like other insects, has three main body divisions: head, thorax, and abdomen. The six legs and four wings that are found in a typical insect are present in a butterfly.

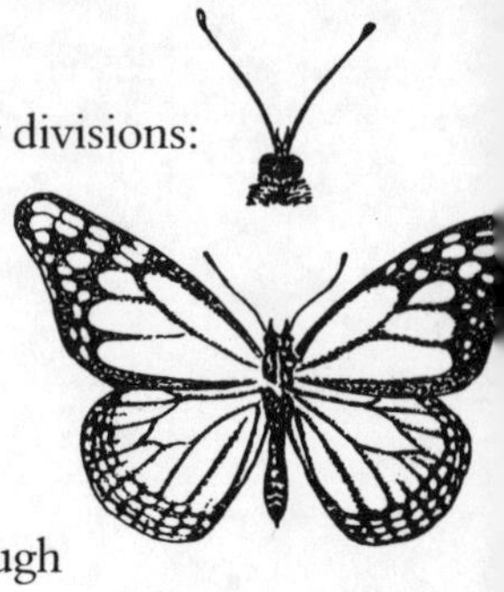

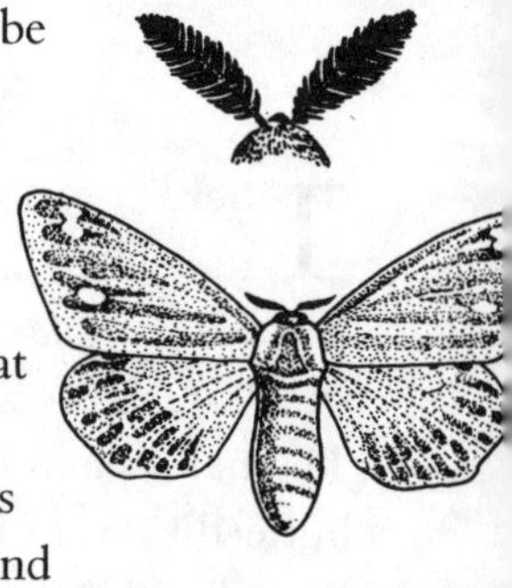

Butterfly and Moth (*antennae magnified*)

BUTTERFLIES AND MOTHS

Silverfish (class Insecta, order Thysanura)

The division of Lepidoptera into moths and butterflies, though convenient, has little scientific validity. The two groups can be differentiated on the basis of several superficial distinctions. Broadly speaking, butterflies fly by day, while moths are active after sunset. There are, of course, several exceptions such as the Evening Brown (*Melanitis leda*) butterfly that flies at dusk. Similarly, there are brightly coloured moths that fly in broad daylight.

When resting, almost all butterflies either fold their wings straight up above their backs, or spread them out sideways and flat, whereas almost all moths fold their wings flat over their backs. Also, a moth's fore and hind wings have a coupling mechanism, like a lobe or spine, that links the wings together during flight.

The antennae (feelers) of a butterfly are plain stalks ending in a club (a hook in the case of Skipper butterflies). Moth antennae are of various patterns but never end in a club.

A butterfly caterpillar always has, besides the three pairs of true legs, five pairs of sucker legs. Many moth caterpillars have less than five pairs of sucker legs, sometimes only two pairs.

LIFE CYCLE OF A BUTTERFLY

The Egg (Ovum; plural, Ova)

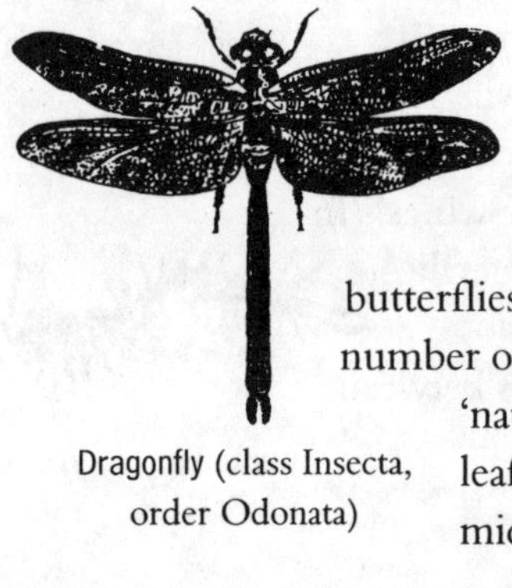

Dragonfly (class Insecta, order Odonata)

Butterfly eggs vary in shape and size according to species. Seen through a microscope, many of them show beautiful colours. A butterfly egg may be shaped like a tall jar or wicker basket, and in some cases, spherical or disc-shaped eggs are also found. A butterfly egg is smaller than the head of a pin.

The egg is laid by a mated female on the food plant. Some butterflies lay their eggs singly, others lay them in groups. Generally, the number of eggs laid by a single female is large, probably to allow for 'nature's wastage'. Being coated with an adhesive, eggs stick to the leaf surface. A minute opening at the top of the egg, called the micropyle, allows air to reach the developing caterpillar inside. It is through this same opening that the egg is fertilized in the female's body. The egg is filled with a nutrient fluid and has a transparent shell that turns pale as the caterpillar develops inside. The caterpillar is visible through the shell just before hatching.

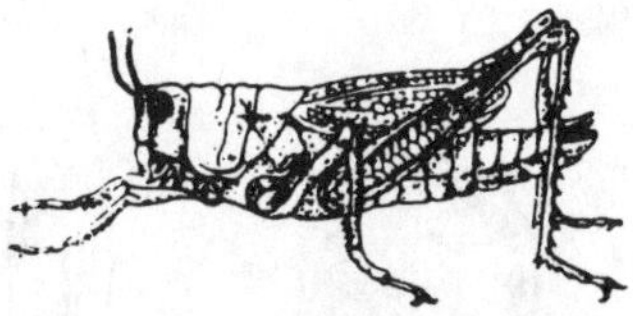

Grasshopper (class Insecta, order Orthoptera)

The Caterpillar (Larva; plural, Larvae)

The caterpillar emerges by biting through the egg-shell, and initially feeds on the empty shell. Thereafter, it feeds only on the leaves of its proper food plant. At first, it just scrapes off the top or underface of the leaf, but once its jaws have grown stronger and larger, it virtually becomes an eating machine, with its jaws moving very rapidly all the time. It demolishes every edible leaf, bud, flower, and shoot that comes in its way. It usually takes semi-circular bites from the edge of the leaf. Such bitten leaves and small droppings on the ground indicate the presence of a caterpillar on a plant. The caterpillars of most butterflies are herbivorous, but a few Lycaenid caterpillars are reported to be carnivorous. Caterpillars of the Brownie (*Gerydus sp.*) feed on aphids whereas the Apefly (*Spalgis epeus*) caterpillar feeds on scale insects like bugs. The caterpillar of the Moth Butterfly (*Liphyra brassolis*) is a most unwelcome guest for tree ants. It not only stays with the ants but also feeds on their larvae.

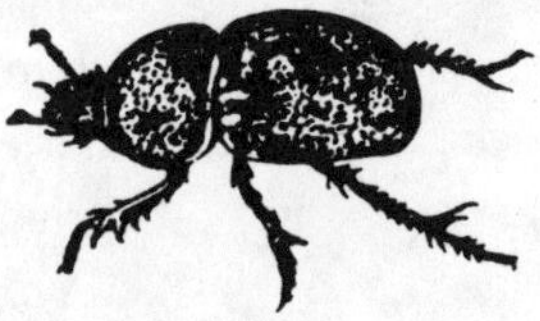

Beetle (class Insecta, order Coleoptera)

Within a few days, the weight of the caterpillar will have increased many times. Sometimes, the food supply is too meagre to permit full growth and since this is the only stage of growth in the butterfly's life cycle, the final result will be a dwarf butterfly if the caterpillar survives the food shortage. While the caterpillar's body grows rapidly, its skin does not grow with the body, but it stretches to accommodate the growing body up to a limit, after which a new layer of skin is formed beneath the old skin. At this stage, the caterpillar temporarily stops eating and comes to rest. The old skin splits behind the head and the larva crawls out of it. Soon after the new skin has hardened, the caterpillar resumes eating, often first devouring the old skin. Such moulting or shedding of the skin takes place five times during the development of the caterpillar. The stage between two sheddings is known as an instar. The newborn caterpillar is counted as the first instar.

Honey bee (class Insecta, order Hymenoptera)

A caterpillar's body is generally shaped like a cigar and is made up of fourteen sections (a head plus thirteen segments). The first three

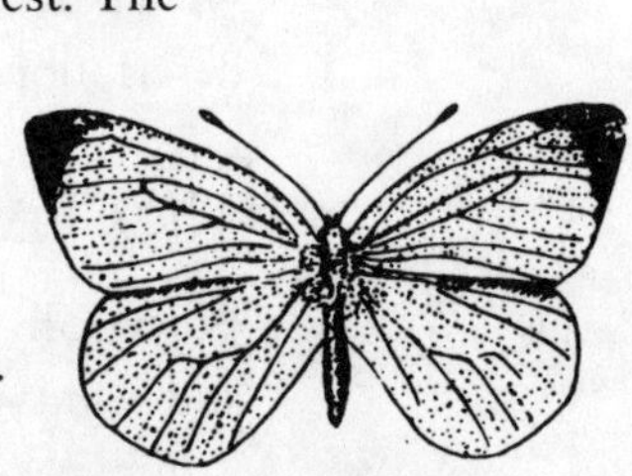

Butterfly (class Insecta, order Lepidoptera)

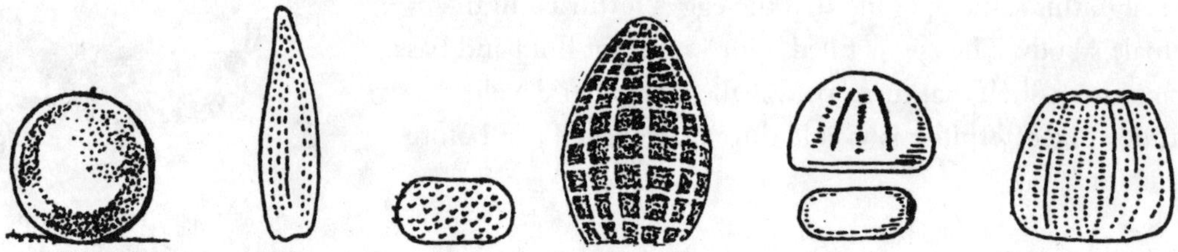

Butterfly eggs

body segments behind the head have a pair each of jointed legs. These three segments make up the thorax. The remaining ten segments form the abdomen, which has five pairs of unjointed, sucker-like, false legs or 'prolegs' that the caterpillar uses to move. The prolegs on the last segment are very strong and hold so firmly to the perch that if the caterpillar is pulled from the head end, it will break into two rather than let go. The heart and nervous system are spread throughout the body. This is the reason why wasps and other enemies have to sting a caterpillar at several places to paralyse it before serving it as food to their young ones.

A caterpillar can neither see nor hear, but it can feel vibrations through the food plant. It can also sense light and darkness through ocelli (simple eyes), which are arranged in two groups of six each, with one group on either side of the head.

Most butterfly caterpillars have smooth bodies. Larvae of some species are decorated with hairs, tufts, or bristles, or they develop certain colours as a device to protect themselves from enemies. The larval stage is the most dangerous period in a butterfly's life. A large number of caterpillars are eaten by birds, lizards, spiders, and the young of hunting wasps. There are other special types of enemies, such as wasps and tachinid flies who lay their eggs on butterfly eggs or inside a living caterpillar. The young parasites that soon hatch from the eggs feed on the butterfly larvae from the inside. The protective devices that caterpillars have developed to deal with their enemies will be described in detail in the butterfly descriptions.

The Chrysalis (Pupa; plural, Pupae)

When fully grown, the caterpillar ceases to feed and begins to wander restlessly. Undigested food is thrown out to clear the digestive tract and the caterpillar becomes almost translucent. Finally, the caterpillar settles down at a suitable spot. It spins a pad

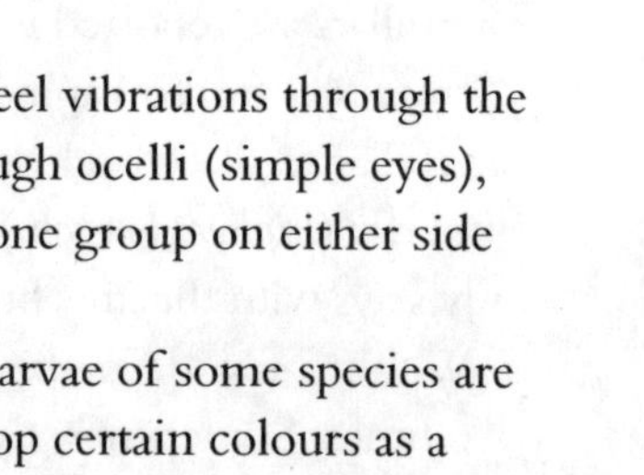
Butterfly (Lepidoptera)

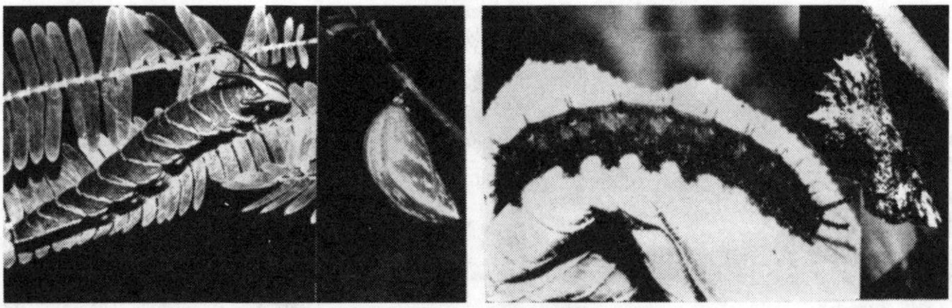

Caterpillars and Pupae

of silk and firmly anchors itself to its perch by its last pair of 'sucker legs'. Many species further support themselves by looping a silken thread around the upper part of the body and attaching both ends to the perch. The caterpillar remains immobile for the next eight to ten hours or even longer, after which it begins to wriggle about while remaining firmly attached to the perch. As it continues to wriggle, the larval skin splits from the top of its head and is worked backwards and discarded. The mouth parts and legs that are no longer needed also go with the skin. The body becomes visibly shorter and stouter and within an hour or two it becomes a recognizable chrysalis or pupa, no longer bearing the least resemblance to a caterpillar. Initially soft and pale, the pupa darkens as it becomes hard. Each type or species forms a pupa of its own peculiar shape and pattern. Some of these look quite strange, but quite a few are very beautiful. A close look at the pupa will reveal the outlines of the main external organs of the future insect, particularly the wings. On the outside, the pupa appears almost lifeless but inside there is great activity and change.

The length of the pupal stage depends on the vegetational season. If the proper food plant is still available, this stage may last for only a few days, usually six to fifteen days. But if the food plants have died, it would be useless for the perfect insect to emerge until the season has come around again. This may perhaps be after several months. Like the larva, the pupa, which is immobile, is also vulnerable to attacks from its enemies. However, pupae develop certain devices which help them to protect themselves. These will be discussed in detail later.

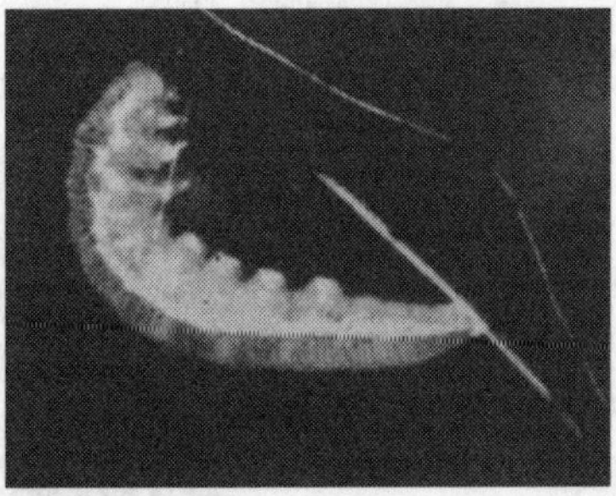

Caterpillar of Common Emigrant butterfly anchored for pupation

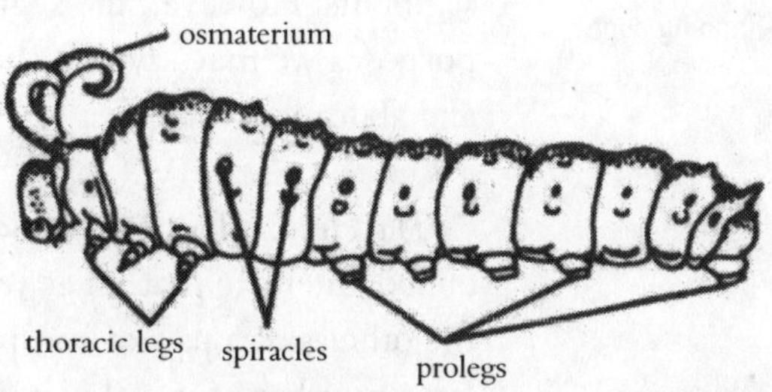

A Caterpillar

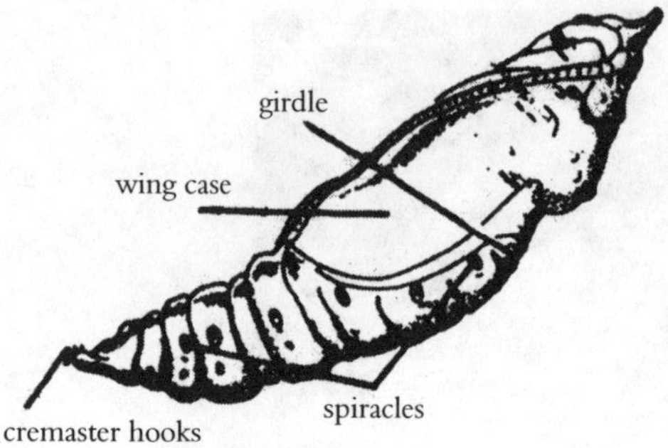

A typical pupa

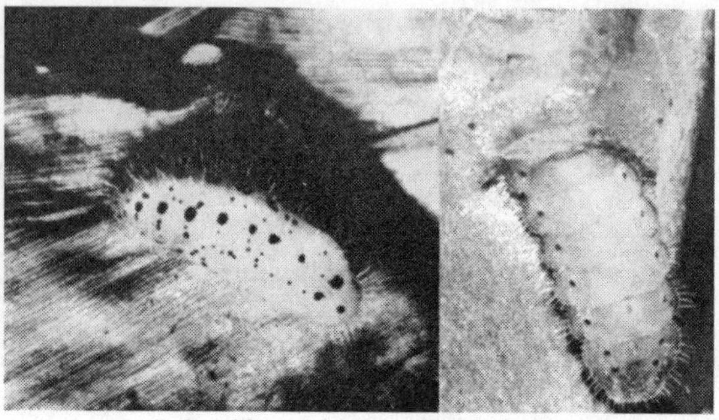
Caterpillar and pupa of Red Pierrot

The Perfect Insect or the Adult Butterfly (Imago; plural, Imagos)

One of the most fascinating sights in nature, which those who have reared caterpillars must have observed, is the emergence of the butterfly from its chrysalis. The pupal case, which becomes transparent, allowing the colours of the butterfly wings to be seen, splits at the head. Waving legs are thrust out and the insect hauls itself clear of the case. It may crawl a few inches to hang on the underside of the stem or leaf to which it was anchored.

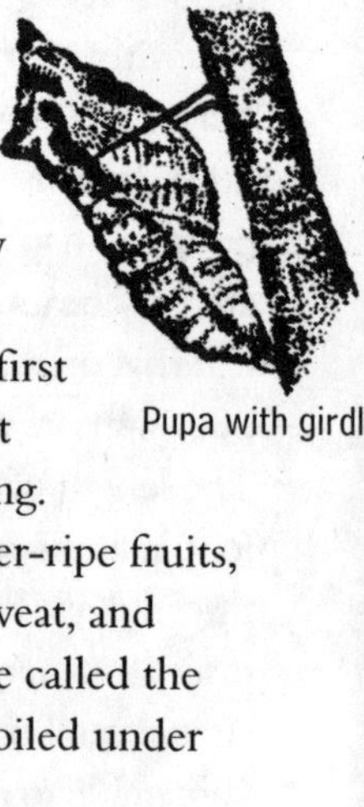
Pupa with girdl

At this point, the wings are shrunken, crumpled, and wet and the abdomen is distended. The wings expand rapidly to their normal size as haemolymph (insect blood) from the abdomen is pumped into the hollow wing veins. The soft wings gradually become stronger after exposure to the air. After resting thus for half an hour or so, the young butterfly (imago) takes to the air, first flapping its wings a few times to get the feel of them. The insect now sets off to begin its activities—searching for food and mating.

Free-hanging pupa

The adult insect consumes only liquids—nectar, juices from over-ripe fruits, oozing plant sap, liquid mud, animal dung and urine, human sweat, and body juices of dead crabs and other animals. A long slender tube called the proboscis helps it in sucking liquids. The tube remains neatly coiled under the head, like a watch spring, when not in use.

The body of the adult butterfly is composed of the head plus thirteen segments. However, the segments are not obvious and for all practical purposes we may say that the perfect insect's body consists of a head, thorax, and abdomen.

The Head: The head carries the following: a pair of club-ended antennae that act as receptors to smell the presence of the other sex, a pair of compound eyes that consist of a large number of visual cones or ommatidia, a long

tubular proboscis made up of two highly modified mouth parts held together by a series of hooks and spikes, rather like a zip-chain, which help in sucking the liquid food, and a pair of sensory pads or palps, one on each side of the antennae, which act as organs of touch.

The size of the eyes is larger in a male butterfly, with more cones present in each eye than in the eye of a female. This is probably because the male needs keener eyesight to seek out the female for courtship and mating.

The Thorax: The head is attached to the thorax by a thin, delicate, short, and membranous neck. The thorax, which looks like a compact structure superficially, is actually composed of three segments that are fused together. Each segment carries a pair of legs on the ventral side.

The legs of butterflies are used for gripping. Each leg has several segments, with a hip joint (coxa) at the base, a thigh (femur), a shank (tibia), and a foot (tarsus), which has five joints, the last having a pair of claws. The foot bears the taste organs and some species have a spur with a brush of hair on the shank which is used to clean the antennae. The fore legs of Nymphalids, Browns, and Milkweed butterflies are imperfectly formed and useless for walking as they are small and clawless. However, in the case of Beaks and Judies, only the male's fore legs are underdeveloped. The fore feet of female Lycaenids have two claws whereas those of males have only one claw.

Each wing of the butterfly is made up of two closely-pressed, thin membranes, supported by a network of 'veins' running between them. The membranes are covered with a number of hollow multiform and multicoloured scales, which determine the coloration of the wings. Each scale has a short stalk which fits into a slot in the wing membrane and the scales overlap like tiles on a roof. The arrangement of the scales forms the pattern of the wing's characteristic markings. The colour is either the result of the

Common Rose emerging from its chrysalis

pigment present in the scale or is due to the presence of ridges and streaks on the scale itself, which breaks up the light that falls on it, causing changes in colour according to the angle from which the wing is viewed. This manifestation of colour (structural colour) is similar to what we see in soap bubbles showing rainbow colours when light passes through them. In butterflies, usually the blue and green colours are produced by structure rather than by pigment. The brilliant iridescence or rainbow effect that some butterflies display is also a result of structural colour. The colours of the undersides of the wings are usually more subdued than those of the upper surfaces. This certainly makes the butterfly less conspicuous when at rest with its wings closed. Males of many species have specialized scent scales called androconia, that differ in shape and structure from normal scales and are attached to a scent gland in the wing membrane from which a scent (pheromone) is emitted during courtship to attract a female. These scent scales are associated with pouches or bands like those seen on the wings of Milkweed butterflies.

In order to describe a butterfly's wing (which is roughly triangular in shape—the hind wing perhaps less so than the fore wing), we need names for all the three sides as well as for the three corners. We also need to name a few areas within the wing's triangle.

Taking first the right-hand fore wing (FW) and going in a clockwise direction from where the wing leaves the thorax, we follow the costa (the leading edge) until we reach the apex (the upper tip of the wing). Coming down from the apex along the termen (the outer edge) we reach the tornus, which is almost a right angle. From the tornus we cut straight back towards the thorax along the dorsum (the lower or trailing edge). The point at which the dorsum joins the thorax is the base. Once you have understood these three sides and three corners in the right FW, you can work them out for the other three wings. In the hind wing (HW), the tornus is of course the lowest point (which may not be a right angle), and the dorsum is the inside edge.

The number, arrangement, and distribution pattern of 'veins' between the

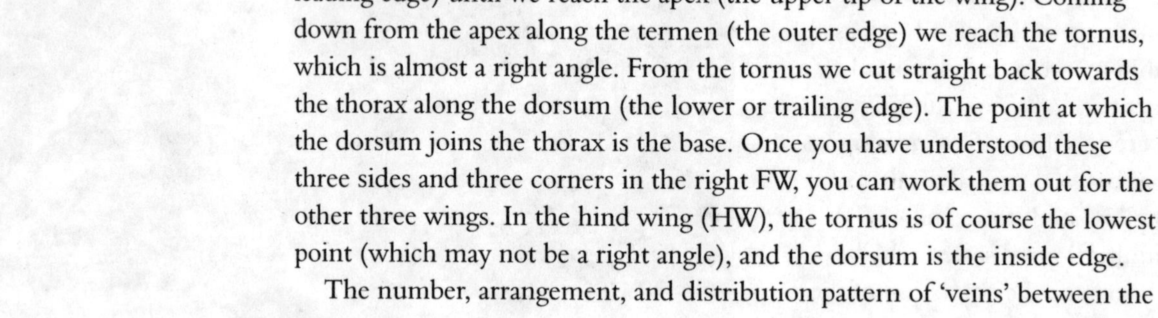

Butterfly Wings

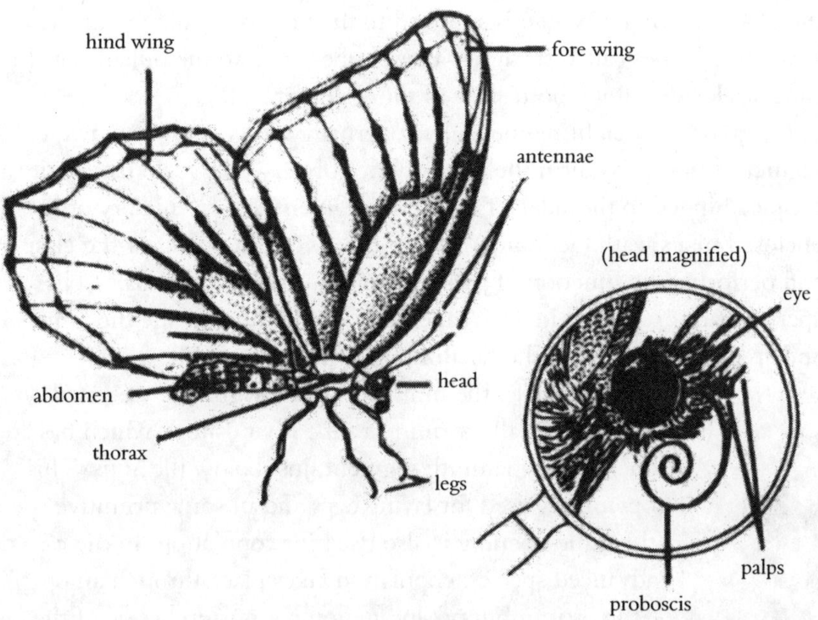

Adult Butterfly

two membranes of a wing varies among different groups of butterflies and is a major tool for their identification and taxonomy. Some ten to twelve, thin black 'veins' spread out from the base across a butterfly's wing. Close to their beginning, these 'veins' leave a comparatively large oblong space empty, which is called the cell. Along the termen lies the 'marginal' area and the part between this and the cell is known as the disc.

The fore wing is reinforced by a costal and sub-costal vein running almost parallel to the outer margin, the costa. The branched veins distributed behind them are known as radial, medial, cubital, and anal.

The movement of the wings is controlled by two sets of internal muscles in the thorax. The wings are raised by the contraction of the thorax by one set of muscles and lowered by the expansion of the thorax by another set. The direction and angle of wings during each stroke is controlled by smaller muscles present directly at the base of the wings.

The Abdomen: An adult butterfly has a cylindrical, slim, and fairly long abdomen. It consists of ten segments that have organs of digestion, respiration, excretion, and reproduction. A butterfly's 'blood' does not flow through veins and arteries, nor does it carry oxygen. Instead, the blood moves freely among the internal organs, supplying nourishment throughout the body. The tubular heart, which is placed along the butterfly's back, keeps the blood moving. Oxygen is supplied to the organs separately through a network of tubes called tracheae. These tubes open to the outside air through spiracles located along both sides of the abdomen.

Only seven or eight segments are externally visible as the last two or three segments modify to form the reproductive organs. The male has a pair of claspers hinged to the sides of the ninth segment. An ejaculatory organ, enclosed in a sheath (aedeagus), is found between the bases of the claspers and performs the function of passing spermatozoa to the female. These spermatozoa are stored in a sac called the spermatheca inside the female body and are later released for the fertilization of the ova.

In the female, the ninth and tenth segments are fused together, usually forming a tube (ovipositor), which has an opening in the ninth segment, just below the anus. This opening is used for laying eggs and in some primitive species the same opening is also used for copulation. In the case of advanced species, copulation takes place through an opening, the ostium bursae, located on the posterior side of the eighth segment. A pair of ovaries, located anteriorly, produce ova, which are then transferred to the ovipositor. En route, the ova are fertilized by the stored spermatozoa, after which they are laid through the posterior opening.

The reproductive organs of butterflies vary in shape among different species. The 'lock-key' type of arrangement of the male and female organs of a species prevents cross-mating between species. These anatomical variations and the complex nature of reproductive organs play a major role in species identification and taxonomy.

The life-span of an adult butterfly can vary from a few weeks to some months, depending on the species. The major task of the butterfly is to propagate its species. Thus, from nature's point of view, a male butterfly that has mated with a female or a female that has laid eggs has fulfilled its biological function. Sometimes, ecological factors such as temperature, availability of food, and suitability of habitat have an impact on the life-span of an adult butterfly.

BUTTERFLY SPECIES

SWALLOWTAILS—THE PAPILIOS

This group contains some of the most spectacular butterflies, ranging from India's largest, the Southern Birdwing, which has a wingspan of up to 190 mm, to the translucent Apollos of the Himalayas, and the quaint little Dragontails of the Northeast. Most species have well-developed, tailed hind wings, hence the name 'Swallowtail'.

Swallowtails can be grouped into commonly known types: True Swallowtails, to which the Lime and the black-bodied Mormons belong; Kite Swallowtails, like the Tailed Jay and Spot Swordtail, which have narrow, pointed, hind wings resembling paper kites; and the poison-eaters, so called because their caterpillars feed on the poisonous Aristolochia creeper, making the subsequent adults a 'protected species'. Examples of poison-eaters are the Crimson Rose and Common Rose (which are mimicked by two forms of the female Common Mormon for survival).

Most Swallowtails lay eggs singly on the growing shoots of the food plant. Their eggs are usually pale yellowish-green, smooth, and spherical, except those of the red-bodied Swallowtails, which are reddish, ribbed, and flat, broadened at the base, and dome-shaped at the top. All Swallowtail caterpillars have a forked organ behind their head that protrudes on alarm and gives off a strong smell to deter predators. Some look like bird-droppings in their early instars. Their food plants are mainly plants related to lime, custard apple, and Aristolochia. *Pupae may be green or mottled brown to resemble a twig and are attached to the perch at an angle at the base, with a silken girdle supporting the pupa in the middle.*

Except the few familiar ones, most Swallowtails are forest dwellers and that is why many of these butterflies are threatened by the destruction of forests. Only about ten countries in the world have significant Swallowtail populations and India is lucky enough to be one of them. About 105 species of Swallowtails, out of the world's 700, are found in India.

Southern Birdwing

SOUTHERN BIRDWING (*TROIDES MINOS*)
WINGSPAN: 140–190 MM

This is the largest Indian butterfly and is closely related to the Golden Birdwing (*Troides aecus*) that flies in the Himalayas from Mussoorie further eastwards. In the Western Ghats, the Southern Birdwing occurs in Goa and further south. It is more commonly seen during the monsoon and immediate post-monsoon months. The best time to see this butterfly is in the early morning, near Lantana bushes.

Common Rose

COMMON ROSE (*PACHLIOPTA ARISTOLOCHIAE*)
WINGSPAN: 80–110 MM (PLATE 8)

This red-bodied Swallowtail is distributed throughout India where it is at home in most types of habitats, except in dense and wet forests. In the northwest of India, its flies up to 3000 feet (*c.* 1000 m). It is migratory and roosts in large numbers together with the Crimson Rose. The caterpillars feed on *Aristolochia indica* in the wild. Garden varieties of *Aristolochia*, however, also attract this butterfly to lay eggs.

Crimson Rose

CRIMSON ROSE (*PACHLIOPTA HECTOR*)
WINGSPAN: 90–110 MM (PLATE 8)

This is an extremely common butterfly in south India and is also found along the east coast in Orissa, south Bihar, and West Bengal. The rows of bright crimson markings on its hind wings and red body are warning signals to avian predators. During the winter months, congregations of thousands of these butterflies roost together in plantations and forest patches, especially in south India. This Swallowtail, too, is migratory.

Common Mime

COMMON MIME (*CHILASA CLYTIA*)
WINGSPAN: 90–100 MM (PLATE 8)

An excellent mimic of the distasteful Blue Tiger and Common Crow, both in appearance and flight, only the series of large yellow spots bordering the underside of the hind wings of this butterfly give it away. The Common Mime is seen frequently, but only in certain localities. In peninsular India, it occurs up to Mumbai and Madhya Pradesh, while in the north, it flies from Kangra (Himachal Pradesh) further eastwards.

LIME BUTTERFLY (*PAPILIO DEMOLEUS*)
WINGSPAN: 80–100 MM (PLATE 2)
This is one of the most widely distributed butterflies. It occurs from southern Iraq through India, up to the Philippines and Australia. It is commonly seen around human dwellings where its favourite food plants, *bael* (*Aegle marmelos*), orange, and lemon, are cultivated. Its caterpillars are very similar to those of the Common Mormon. The pale yellow markings on the wings turn to deep orange as the butterfly ages. The dry season brings hundreds of these butterflies to damp patches for mudpuddling.

Common Mormon

COMMON MORMON (*PAPILIO POLYTES*)
WINGSPAN: 90–100 MM
This common Swallowtail occurs near human habitations, especially where curry-leaf plants, oranges, and lemons are cultivated. The female Mormon exists in three colour forms; in two of these forms, it mimics two red-bodied Swallowtails, the Common Rose and the Crimson Rose, and in the third form, it resembles the male. Caterpillars initially appear like fresh bird droppings and are green in the last instar.

BLUE MORMON (*PAPILIO POLYMNESTOR*) WINGSPAN: 120–150 MM (PLATE 2)
This is the second-largest Swallowtail of peninsular India, where it occurs in heavily forested regions up to Mumbai and Madhya Pradesh, and north-eastwards to south Bihar and West Bengal. In the north, its equal-sized cousin, the Great Mormon, *Papilio memnon*, replaces it from Bengal and Sikkim onwards. It is common practically everywhere in wooded hill-stations, where it may be seen in swift, dipping flight, the pale blue of its hind wings flashing.

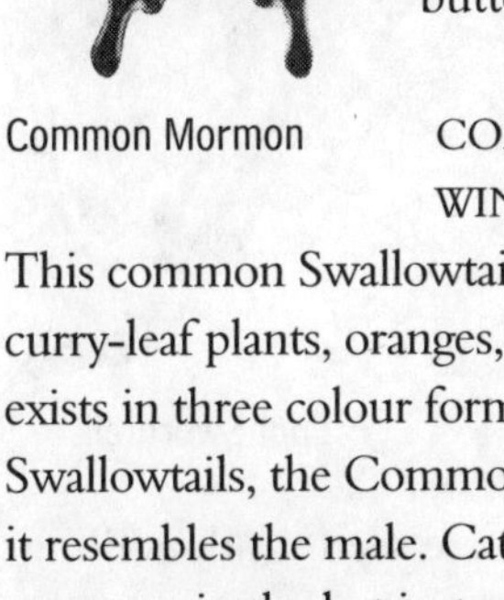

Common Bluebottle

COMMON BLUEBOTTLE (*GRAPHIUM SARPEDON*)
WINGSPAN: 80–90 MM (PLATE 2)
This handsome butterfly has a pale blue or greenish band running across the middle of its

Tailed Jay

black wings on both the sides. The hind wings on both sides have tiny green crescents near the border. This butterfly is easily noticed both when it flies swiftly with a skipping motion, flashing its blue-green colours and when it mudpuddles on damp patches along with other butterflies. It is seen in and around the wooded regions of south India and in the Himalayas from Kashmir further eastwards.

TAILED JAY (*GRAPHIUM AGAMEMNON*) WINGSPAN: 85–100 MM (PLATE 2)
A restless flier in city gardens, it is quite common in spite of being essentially a butterfly of wooded country. Its recent abundance in cities is mainly due to the wide-scale popularity of its favourite food plant, the Mast Tree or false Ashok (*Polyalthia longifolia*). It is confined to heavy rainfall areas ranging from South India up to the forested regions of south Gujarat and also flies from Kumaon eastwards.

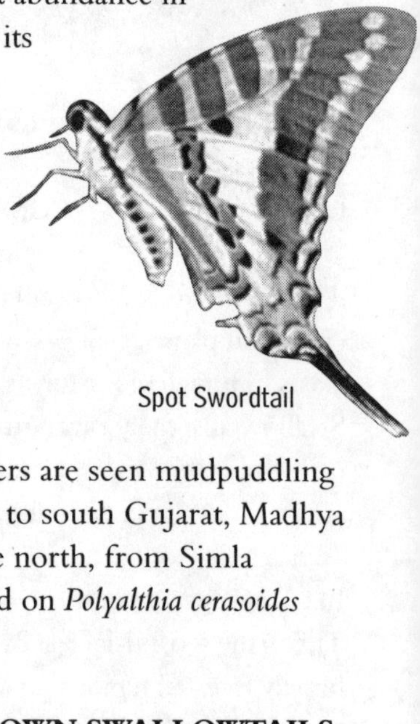
Spot Swordtail

SPOT SWORDTAIL (*PATHYSA NOMIUS*)
WINGSPAN: 75–90 MM (PLATE 2)
This is chiefly a butterfly of dry, mixed, and deciduous forests, where in summer, large numbers are seen mudpuddling on damp patches. It ranges from peninsular India to south Gujarat, Madhya Pradesh, south Bihar, and West Bengal, and in the north, from Simla further eastwards. Its caterpillars feed on *Polyalthia cerasoides* and *Milusa tomentosa*.

Kaiser-i-Hind

SOME RARE AND LESSER KNOWN SWALLOWTAILS

KAISER-I-HIND (*TEINOPALPUS IMPERIALIS*)
WINGSPAN: 90–120 MM
A truly handsome butterfly, besides being one of the rarest, it is found in the wooded hills (6000–10,000 feet or *c.* 2000–3500 m) of Northeast India from Sikkim eastwards. Unlike most Swallowtails, flowers hold no attraction for this butterfly. For butterfly collectors the world over, this is one of the most prized butterflies.

Bhutan Glory

BHUTAN GLORY (*BHUTANITIS LIDDERDALEI*)
WINGSPAN: 90–110 MM

Another rare butterfly that is known to occur in Bhutan and further northeast, where it flies in the hills from 5000 to 9000 feet (*c.* 1700–3000 m), is the Bhutan Glory. It has two breeding seasons, one in May–June and another in August–October. Very little is known about its early stages of growth. However, it is suspected to lay eggs on wild *Aristolochia* and hence is distasteful to predators.

WHITE DRAGONTAIL (*LAMPROPTERA CURIUS*) WINGSPAN: 40–50 MM

Dragontails are quaint looking butterflies that have transparent black-banded fore wings and enormously long-tailed hind wings. In flight, they often resemble dragonflies. While mudpuddling, they can be seen squirting out water from the rear end. They are confined to the northeastern jungles of India from Assam onwards. Not much is known about their early stages.

White Dragontail

The White Dragontail is a swift flier of open jungles, where it may be seen feeding while hovering over flowers without settling on them. A white band that runs across both the wings in the basal region distinguishes it from the closely related Green Dragontail (*L. meges*; Wingspan: 40–55 mm), which has a greenish band.

COMMON BLUE APOLLO (*PARNASSIUS HARDWICKII*)
WINGSPAN: 50–65 MM

Snow Apollos are frail-looking butterflies, but survive in harsh weather conditions. They dwell in the mighty Himalayas, most of them rarely descending below 12,000 feet (*c.* 4000 m). Apollos may not be as rare as they are thought to be, but since many of them dwell in the remote inaccessible mountain valleys and passes, very little is known about them. Several species of Apollos occur in alpine heights from the western Himalayas Northeast India.

The Common Blue Apollo is the commonest among the Apollos. It may be seen in the hills as low as 8000 feet and can be

Common Blue Apollo

noticed almost all through the year. Its flight is rapid but it flutters close to the ground and frequently settles on flowers to feed. As in all Apollos, females develop a horny pouch on mating, formed by the quick-drying substance discharged by the male to prevent further mating. Caterpillars are known to feed on *Saxifrage sp*. Pupation takes place in a loose cocoon among leaf litter or even underground.

WHITES AND YELLOWS—THE PIERIDS

These are basically white, yellow, or orange butterflies, often with black markings. Some, like Jezebels, have striking colours. The word 'butterfly' could possibly have originated from the butter-yellow colour of some of these butterflies, especially the male Brimstone butterfly. In Europe, Brimstones are the first butterflies to appear with the arrival of spring. The Brimstone is also common in the Himalayan foothills.

The majority of these butterflies are sun-worshippers and quickly withdraw into the foliage if a cloud obscures the sun. In the summer, several species are seen mudpuddling in large numbers on damp patches. All Pierids have a great affinity to flowers. A prominent feature of this group is their strong migratory habit. At times, many millions of Lemon Emigrants have been seen flying together in one direction. These flights may continue intermittently for several days with the butterflies resting in clusters at night in a sheltered plantation or forest patch and resuming their flight the next morning.

Pierid eggs are usually laid singly on the upper or underside of leaves or shoots. Some, like Jezebels and Pioneers, however, lay their eggs in clusters and their caterpillars too live together. The caterpillars are well-camouflaged and when alarmed, they spew out a green, unpleasant-smelling liquid from their mouth, and flick their heads. Despite this, parasitic flies and ichneumon wasps take their toll on them, and the potter wasps too feed their grubs on Pierid caterpillars.

The pupae are attached to their perch by a tail hook and are supported by a central girdle. The pupae remain below the leaf, either parallel or hanging at an angle to it. They are usually pointed at both ends with wing cases producing a pronounced keel.

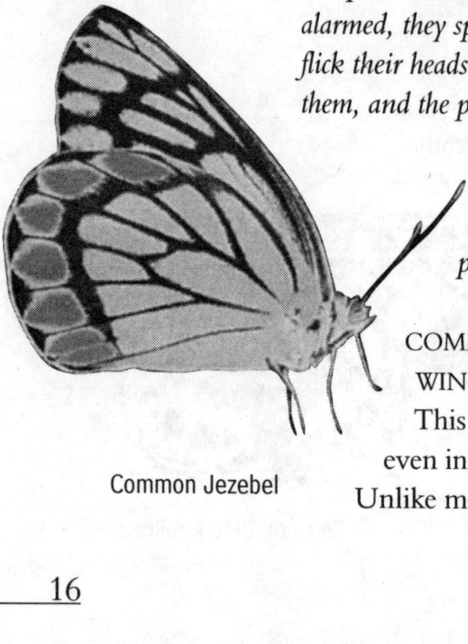

Common Jezebel

COMMON JEZEBEL (*DELIAS EUCHARIS*)
WINGSPAN: 66–83 MM (PLATE 3)

This is one of the most striking butterflies and is sometimes seen even in the middle of busy city roads, with its lazy, mincing flight. Unlike most butterflies, the Common Jezebel has bright colours on the undersides of the wings as well, which warn predators to keep off. This butterfly is quite distasteful due to plant poisons derived from its food plant, *Dendrophthoe sp.*, a mistletoe-like parasite. When attacked, it feigns death. It is common throughout India, except in the arid zones. The Painted Sawtooth (*Prioneris sita*) mimics this butterfly.

PSYCHE (*LEPTOSIA NINA*) WINGSPAN: 35–50 MM
The weakest flier among this group, it is often seen flapping incessantly about the undergrowth, within a range of up to 1 metre above grass level. It is quite common throughout India wherever its food plant, Caper (*Capparis sp.*) grows.

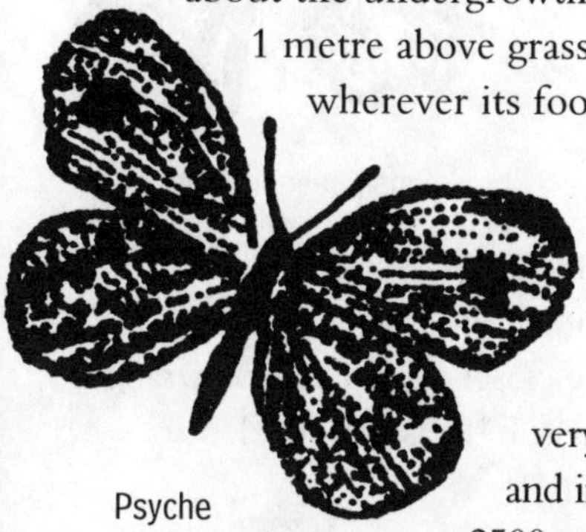
Psyche

INDIAN CABBAGE WHITE (*PIERIS CANIDIA*)
WINGSPAN: 45–60 MM
As its name suggests, this is one of the pests attacking cabbages. In the southern hills, it is very common above 5400 feet (1800 m) and in the Himalayas, it flies from 2500 to about 11,000 feet (*c.* 800–4000 m). In the north, this butterfly, being a regular migrant, descends from the hills onto the plains in winter, and returns to the hills with the onset of spring. It is a low-flying butterfly that frequents shrubs and bushes, but keeps out of forests.

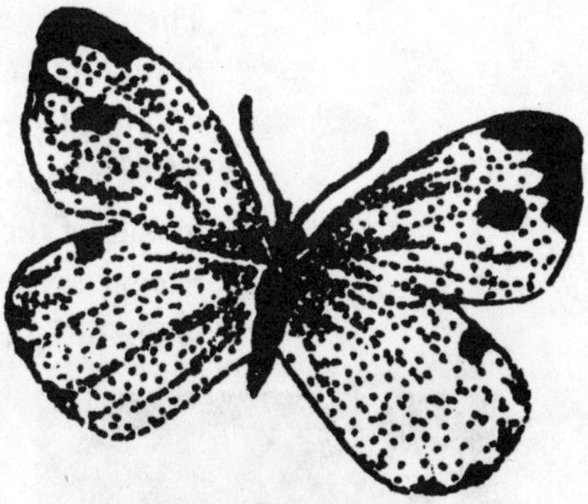
Indian Cabbage White

COMMON GULL (*CEPORA NERISSA*)
WINGSPAN: 40–65 MM (PLATE 3)
This is one of the most common butterflies, occurring throughout India. It is seen on the wing all through the year, except where the winter is extremely severe. It is very fond of flowers. On hot summer days, large numbers of this species may be seen mudpuddling on damp patches. It is a butterfly mainly of the warmer regions where its food plant Caper (*Capparis sp.*) grows.

Common Gull

PIONEER (*ANAPHAEIS AUROTA*)
WINGSPAN: 40–55 MM (PLATE 3)
This sun-loving fast flier is at home in open, dry country throughout India, except for Assam and eastwards. In the Himalayas, it flies up to 8500 feet

Pioneer

(*c.* 2800 m). Seen throughout the year, except where summers and winters are extreme, it is known to migrate in large swarms.

SMALL SALMON ARAB (*COLOTIS AMATA*)
WINGSPAN: 35–50 MM

This is a salmon pink butterfly of dry, semi-arid, scrub and thorn forest. It ranges throughout India except in the Northeast. It usually flies close to the ground and is rarely seen on flowers. The grey-barked evergreen, *Salvadora*, that grows in dry and saline lands, is its favourite food plant, besides *Azima sp*. Its caterpillars are gregarious.

Small Salmon Arab

WHITE ORANGE TIP (*IXIAS MARIANNE*) WINGSPAN: 50–55 MM (PLATE 3)
YELLOW ORANGE TIP (*IXIAS PYRENE*) WINGSPAN: 50–70 MM (PLATE 3)

The White Orange Tip is less common than the closely-allied Yellow Orange Tip, though the distribution of both the species in India is almost identical. They have common food plants and may be found mudpuddling together on damp patches. The White Orange Tip prefers open plains and scrub country while the other is more at home in scrub along the hill ranges. The female of the Yellow Orange Tip differs from its male by having a white band in place of an orange one. It is normally white or light yellow with black markings. The female of the White Orange Tip has black spots in its apical orange patch.

Yellow Orange Tip

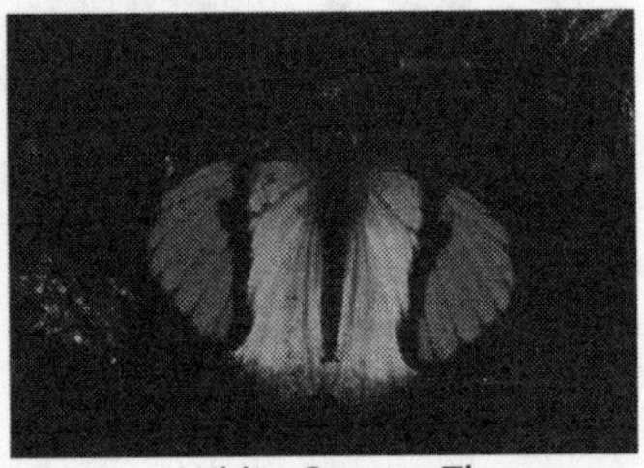

White Orange Tip

GREAT ORANGE TIP (*HEBOMOIA GLAUCIPPE*)
WINGSPAN: 80–100 MM (PLATE 3)

This is the largest butterfly among the Whites and is a powerful flier. Its black-edged orange tips marked against white make it a conspicuous insect in flight, but while mudpuddling in a group, the fore wings are folded back between the hind wings, so that only the protective mottled red or brown markings on the undersides of the hind wings, and the fore wing tips are seen. The camouflage pattern of its underside renders this butterfly almost invisible among fallen leaves and stones. Its tall, bottle-shaped, white eggs are laid singly on Capers. Its caterpillar, when alarmed, rears its head and flattens

Yellow Orange Tip (*Fema*

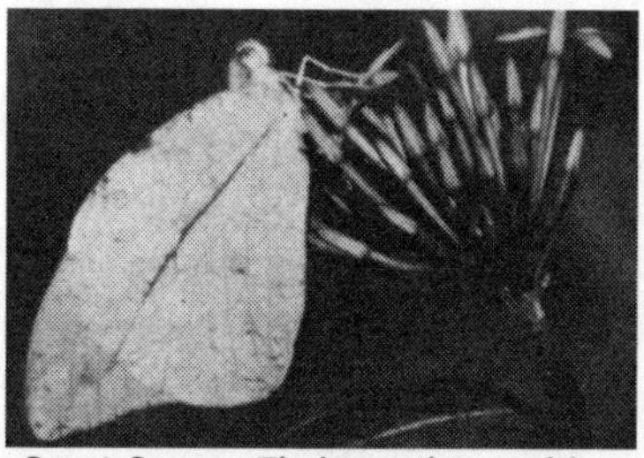

Great Orange Tip in resting position

its sides to reveal blue and yellow eye-spots. This gives it a snake-like appearance.

COMMON WANDERER
(*PARERONIA VALERIA*)
WINGSPAN: 65–80 MM (PLATE 3)

With pale blue and black margins on its wings, this butterfly could be mistaken for the Blue Tiger. In fact, the female is an effective mimic of this Milkweed butterfly. It is common throughout India and prefers open forests with moderate rainfall. A swift-flying butterfly that is often seen on flowers or basking in the morning sun, it lays its eggs on Capers.

Great Orange Tip

COMMON OR LEMON EMIGRANT (*CATOPSILIA POMONA*)
WINGSPAN: 55–80 MM (PLATE 3)

Powerful fliers and well-known migrants, swarms of these butterflies (in thousands) have been seen flying in a particular direction. Their colour varies from pale yellow to white; males are sulphur-yellow at the base of their wings. There are two main colour forms: the crocale form has black antennae and its undersides are without any markings, while the pomona form has reddish antennae and the undersides have silvery red-ringed spots at the end of the cell. These butterflies are fond of flowers and may also be seen mudpuddling in large numbers.

Common Wanderer (*Male*)

MOTTLED EMIGRANT (*CATOPSILIA PYRANTHE*)
WINGSPAN: 50–70 MM

Common and Mottled Emigrants appear almost identical, unless seen at close quarters. Colours vary from chalky white to green. This butterfly too occurs in two forms. The florella form has a very narrow border on the upperside of the fore wings and distinct red-ringed silver spots on the underside at the end cell. The pyranthe form has the underside of its hind wings closely mottled with fine brown or green lines. This butterfly is a strong migrant and may be found mudpuddling in large numbers.

Common Wanderer (*Female*)

Common Emigrant

COMMON GRASS YELLOW (*EUREMA HECABE*)
WINGSPAN: 40–50 MM (PLATE 1)

This butterfly is the commonest among the six species of Grass Yellows that are found in India. Though often seen flying weakly over grass patches, this small, fragile insect has nothing to do with grass. Its food plants are *Cassia* and other legumes. It is on the wing throughout the year, except when winters are extreme. It is often seen on garden flowers and mudpuddling on damp patches.

BLUES—THE LYCAENIDS

Although the predominant colour of these relatively small butterflies is blue, they come in almost all colours, and some of them are brilliantly iridescent, especially the males. Many have their hind wings tailed or lobed, or both, and in addition, they have prominent eyespots. While resting or feeding, these butterflies intermittently rub their hind wings, which causes their tails to move. This gives enemies the impression that the head is at the rear end. This diversionary tactic seems to meet with success as these butterflies are often seen with their wing lobes and tails snipped off.

*Lycaenids lay turban or dome-shaped, white or pale green eggs singly on growing shoots, flower buds, pods, or near the food plant. The eggs are well-hidden when laid. Those butterflies whose caterpillars are attended by ants will make sure of the presence of ants on the food plant before laying eggs. Where the climate is extreme, certain species pass the winter in the egg stage and hatch during spring. The flattish, slug-like caterpillars keep a low profile on the food plant and are, therefore, not easily seen. The association of caterpillars of certain Lycaenids with ants who protect them is one of the most interesting examples of symbiotic behaviour in the insect world. These caterpillars have specialized organs on their rear segments, which the ants stroke with their antennae for a reward of tiny droplets of sweet liquid from the organ. With this incentive, the ants remain in constant attendance on the caterpillar and protect it, especially from parasitic flies and wasps. For caterpillars of the Dark Pierrot (*Castalius ananda*), tree ants (*Crematogaster sp.*) build small shelters in which the caterpillars take refuge during moulting. The ants escort the caterpillars as they proceed to pupate in the bark crevices. The pupae too are guarded till the butterfly emerges.*

COMMON PIERROT (*CASTALIUS ROSIMON*) WINGSPAN: 24–32 MM
Black spots and streaks on white wings make this butterfly a conspicuous insect. It is usually seen fluttering around its food plant, *ber* or Jujube. It is common in most parts of India, except in the arid north. Besides perching on

Zebra Blue

flowers, it is also seen on bird-droppings and dead insects. On hot days, this butterfly may be seen mudpuddling along with other butterflies.

ANGLED PIERROT (*CALETA CALETA*)
WINGSPAN: 26–32 MM
This butterfly is more partial to wooded country where the rainfall is good. It usually keeps to sheltered clearings and shady streams where it may be seen either on damp patches, flowers, or bird-droppings. It occurs in suitable habitats in peninsular India up to Madhya Pradesh, in West Bengal, Sikkim, and even further eastwards.

ZEBRA BLUE (*SYNTARUCUS PLINIUS*)
WINGSPAN: 22–30 MM (PLATE 4)
Though common throughout India, this butterfly is more at home in drier regions. It is a strong flier that is often seen chasing its own kind. Its food plants are various legumes like *sirish* (*Albizzia*) or *Sebania*. *Plumbago* or *chitrak*, which is suspected to be an insectivorous-plant, is surprisingly its favourite. It is more conspicuous during the drier months.

Pale Grass Blue

PALE GRASS BLUE (*PSEUDOZIZEERIA MAHA*)
WINGSPAN: 26–30 MM (PLATE 4)
Widely distributed in India, this butterfly is the largest among the Grass Blues. The male has pale blue dark-bordered wings on the upperside, whereas the female is dark brown with more or less blue scaling in the basal area of the wings on the upperside. It is more abundant during post-monsoon months.

LIME BLUE (*CHILADES LAIUS*) WINGSPAN: 26–30 MM (PLATE 4)
Wherever limes and oranges are grown, this small butterfly is a common sight. Its tiny caterpillar remains among the young shoots on which it feeds with ants who keep it company. It is active in the sunshine and fond of flowers. As with other butterflies of this group, this butterfly has to be seen at close quarters for proper identification.

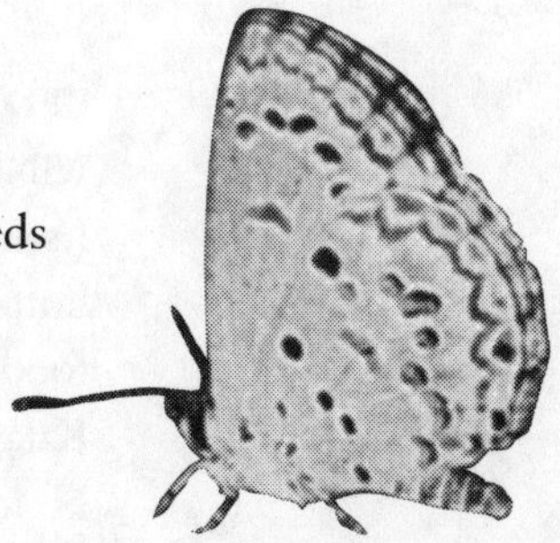

Lime Blue

GRASS JEWEL (*FREYERIA TROCHILUS*) WINGSPAN: 15–22 MM
The smallest of Indian butterflies, it is common throughout the country and may be seen fluttering among low-growing plants. It is tail-less, with a row

Grass Jewel

of jewelled, metallic, orange-crowned spots bordering the undersides of its hind wings.

GRAM BLUE (*EUCHRYSOPS CNEJUS*)
WINGSPAN: 25–33 MM (PLATE 4)

Notwithstanding its size, this exceptionally strong flier is often seen on flowers or basking in the sun with half-open wings. With wings closed, the undersides of the hind wings show two well-separated spots near the tornus. It does occur in the gram fields as a minor pest, but usually prefers to lay eggs on wild legumes. It is widespread throughout India.

Gram Blue

PEA BLUE (*LAMPIDES BOETICUS*) WINGSPAN: 24–36 MM

Pea Blue

In Britain and Europe, it is called the Long-tailed Blue. However, in India, it is not called by that name, since there are several Blues with longer tails. This small butterfly is a persistent migrant, which is probably the reason for its wide distribution all around the world. It is found in Africa, Europe, Asia, Australia, and Hawaii. It is common throughout India and when we are shelling peas, we often find its caterpillars in the pods. In the hills, it is found up to 10,000 feet.

COMMON CERULEAN (*JAMIDES CELENO*)
WINGSPAN: 27–40 MM (PLATE 4)

It is one of the commonest among the Lycaenids and occurs throughout India in every type of habitat, especially where its preferred food plants, *karanj* or *pongam,* and Flame of the Forest or *palas,* are found. It is often seen flying around low bushes for considerable lengths of time before settling. Ants protect its caterpillars with great zeal.

RED PIERROT (*TALICADA NYSEUS*)
WINGSPAN: 30–36 MM (PLATE 4)

Its unusual and striking colour pattern is unmistakable. This butterfly is a weak flier and is always within close range of its food plant. Its caterpillars tunnel within the fleshy leaves of Kalanchoe and Bryophyllum, and the pale yellow pupae may be seen on the leaves. It is found throughout peninsular India up to Mumbai and Orissa, and in Northeast India.

Common Cerulean

Red Pierrot

LARGE OAKBLUE (*ARHOPALA AMANTES*)
WINGSPAN: 45–57 MM
Oakblues are a sizeable group among the Lycaenids, having the largest and some of the most beautiful butterflies. The males are brilliant blue or purple with dark borders on the uppersides, while the females are paler with the wing borders being much broader. Their undersides are in shades of grey and brown with spots or bands. The hind wings of most Oakblues have tails. Basically, they are forest insects and may, at the most, be seen at forest edges or clearings. Flowers do not fascinate them but they may be seen on bird-droppings, carrion, and damp patches.

The Large Oakblue is a brilliant butterfly when seen flying, the shining metallic blue of its black-bordered upperside flashing as it moves. Its undersides are in sober shades of grey-brown with dark spots and bands of spots. It is common in the Indian peninsula up to Madhya Pradesh and south Bihar. In the north, it flies in the Himalayan foothills below 5000 feet (*c.* 1700 m) from Uttar Pradesh further eastwards. Flowers hold no attraction for this butterfly but injured tree stems that exude sugary sap and damp patches are its favourite haunts.

COMMON ACACIA BLUE (*SURENDRA QUERCETORUM*)
WINGSPAN: 30–40 MM
This drab butterfly is often seen at the nectar glands of *Acacia* leaflets, sharing the juices with ants. The male is violet on the upperside and has one pair of tails on the hind wings. The female is brown with two pairs of tails on the hind wings. This is a butterfly of well-forested regions with fairly heavy rainfall and is common along the Western Ghats and in the east up to south Bihar. In the north, it ranges from the Simla hills onwards. The flat, slug-like caterpillars are green with silvery stripes and are looked after by ants on the *Acacia* tree.

LEAF BLUE (*HORSFIELDIA ANITA*)
WINGSPAN: 45–52 MM (PLATE 4)
The shape and underside patterns of this butterfly resemble a leaf. A larger version is the Blue Oakleaf Kallima. So much does it rely on this camouflage, that it stays still when approached, till almost touched. A fast flier, it keeps to forested

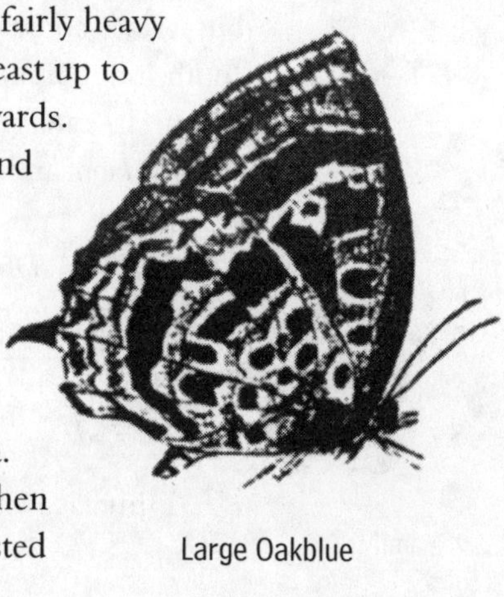

Large Oakblue

Leaf Blue

regions of peninsular India up to Madhya Pradesh, through West Bengal, Assam, and further eastwards. Males are deep purple or blue with a black border on the uppersides, while females are dark brown with bright purple discal areas.

COMMON SILVERLINE (*SPINDASIS VULCANUS*)
WINGSPAN: 26–34 MM (PLATE 4)
While the silver streaks in broad bands on the undersides of this butterfly are unmistakable, some species of Silverlines are very alike, with only minor differences. This butterfly frequents open country and occurs all over India, except in the arid regions of the northwestern part of the country. The caterpillars are always well-attended by Crematogaster ants and therefore their choice of food plant always depends on the presence of ants. The adult is a fast flier and visits garden flowers.

Common Silverline

YAMFLY (*LOXURA ATYMNUS*)
WINGSPAN: 36–40 MM (PLATE 4)
This is a resident of bamboo jungles where its food plants, wild yam (*Dioscorea*) and *Smilax*, grow. It is found in South India, Madhya Pradesh, Orissa, south Bihar, and West Bengal. In the Himalayas, it flies from Mussoorie further eastwards. It keeps to sheltered forest edges and avoids open places. Its caterpillars are looked after by the fierce red ants.

MONKEY PUZZLE (*RATHINDA AMOR*) WINGSPAN: 26–28 MM (PLATE 4)
This butterfly of retiring habits usually keeps to bushes growing in the shade, but it does come to bask at forest edges. It is confined to forests and scrub in south India, along the Western and Eastern Ghats, Orissa, West Bengal, and Assam. Its caterpillar has pointed, fleshy tubercles like those of the Monkey Puzzle. *Ixora* and *kusum* (*Schleichera sp.*) are its preferred food plants.

CORNELIAN (*DEUDORYX EPIJARBAS*) WINGSPAN: 34–44 MM
This is one of those Lycaenids whose caterpillars feed inside fruits, thus remaining hidden till the imagos emerge. It is a strong flier common throughout India, except in dry, desert-like regions. It is at home both in forests and in the open plains. In the Himalayas, it is seen up to 7000 feet (*c.* 2300 m). Though several wild,

Yamfly

PLATE 1

Caterpillar | Pupa | Adult

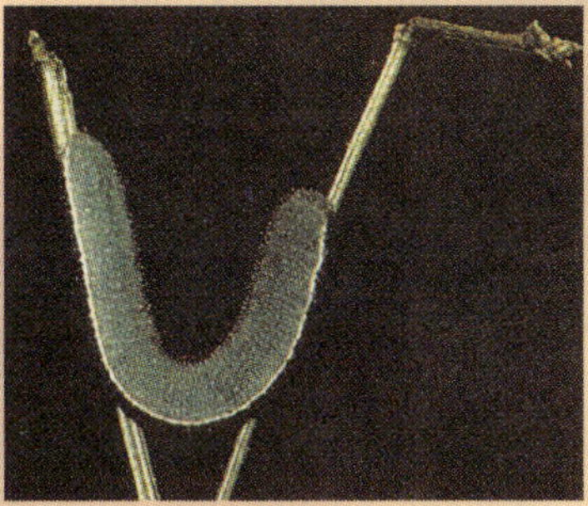

Common Grass Yellow

Common Indian Crow

Common Evening Brown

Common Baron

PLATE 2: Swallowtails and Milkweed Butterflies

Lime Butterfly

Common Bluebottle

Tailed Jay

Blue Tiger

Spot Swordtail

Glassy Tiger

Blue Mormon

Striped Tiger

PLATE 3: Yellows and Whites

Common Jezebel

Yellow Orange Tip

Common Gull

Great Orange Tip

Pioneer

Common Wanderer

White Orange Tip

Common Emigrant

PLATE 4: Blues

Zebra Blue

Common Cerulean

Yamfly

Pale Grass Blue

Red Pierrot

Monkey Puzzle

Lime Blue

Leaf Blue

Indian Red Flash

Gram Blue

Common Silverline

Plum Judy

PLATE 5

Browns

Skippers

Bamboo Treebrown

Common Banded Awl

Grass Demon

Dark Brand Bushbrown

Brown Awl

Common Redeye

Nigger

Malabar Spotted Flat

Dark Palm Dart

Common Fivering

Golden Angle

Conjoined Swift

PLATE 6: Nymphalids

Joker

Yellow Pansy

Leopard

Angled Castor

Indian Fritillary

Painted Lady

Blue Pansy

Peacock Pansy

PLATE 7: Nymphalids

Indian Tortoiseshell

Baronet

Danaid Eggfly (male)

Common Nawab

Blue Oakleaf

Tawny Rajah

Map Butterfly

Tawny Coster

PLATE 8: Mimicry

Models

Mimics

Common Rose

Common Mormon (female)

Crimson Rose

Common Mormon (female)

Plain Tiger

Danaid Eggfly (female)

Blue Tiger

Common Mime

fruit-bearing trees are preferred by it for egg-laying, pomegranate orchards are its favourite haunts. The female is often much larger than the male.

Monkey Puzzle

INDIAN RED FLASH (*BASPA MELAMPUS*)
WINGSPAN: 33–38 MM (PLATE 4)
Flashes form another large group of robust little butterflies that come in shades of red, brown, purple, or blue. On the undersides, they have a bar at the end of each cell and a band across the discal area of both the wings. Their lobed hind wings are tailed with a spot. This group is widely distributed in India, especially in the forested regions. They are fond of flowers and may be seen mudpuddling too.

The Indian Red Flash is found almost throughout India, except in the Northeast and the arid northwestern parts. It is more common on the plains. The male is red, with a purple sheen on the upperside, having a narrow black border all along its fore wings, but not along the dorsum. Its hind wings are all red. The female is a paler version. Undersides of both the sexes are slate grey and the spot on the hind wings is not prominently orange-crowned.

Indian Red Flash

INDIAN SUNBEAM (*CURETIS THETIS*) WINGSPAN: 40–48 MM
This strong flier is an insect of the scrub jungle, where its favourite food plants karanj or pongam grow. Though not easily seen, it is the commonest among the four species of Sunbeams that are found in India. It occurs in suitable habitats in peninsular India, south Gujarat, Madhya Pradesh, and West Bengal, and in some parts of Northeast India. The female has black and white markings on the uppersides, while the male is orange with a narrow black border on the upper and outer margins of its wings. Flowers do not attract this butterfly but bird-droppings do. Its caterpillars have two pillar-like structures from which, on alarm, long tentacles come out with brush-like heads that open into rosettes of hair. These hair-bearing tentacles are whirled rapidly, possibly to scare away parasitic wasps and flies.

(*Male*)

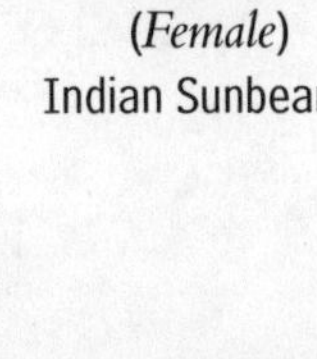
(*Female*)
Indian Sunbeams

MOTH BUTTERFLY (*LIPHYRA BRASSOLIS*) WINGSPAN: 86–92 MM
A rare oddity that appears more moth-like, this stout butterfly occurs from Sikkim further east and can be seen in the mornings and evenings. Its caterpillars live with fierce red

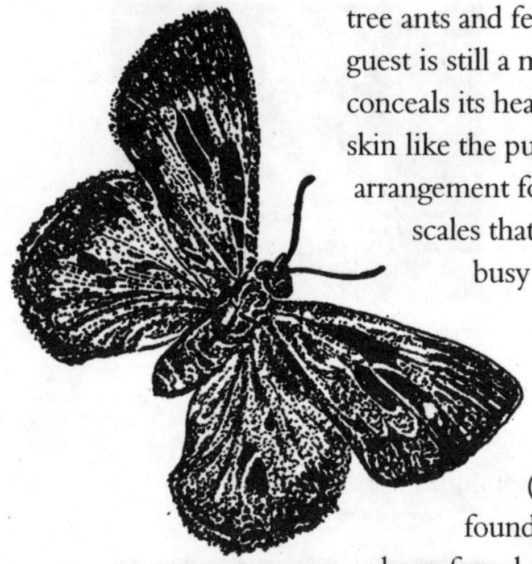

Moth Butterfly

tree ants and feed on the ant larvae. How the ants tolerate this unwelcome guest is still a mystery. Of course, the caterpillar has a tough skin that also conceals its head and legs. Even on pupation, it does not cast off this tough skin like the pupae of other butterflies and moths do. This is probably its arrangement for protection from ants. Also, the imago is covered with loose scales that can come off easily and which are adhesive to keep the ants busy while the butterfly makes its escape.

PLUM JUDY (*ABISARA ECHERIUS*) WINGSPAN: 40–50 MM (PLATE 4)

Earlier, the Judies and Punches were put with the Beaks (*Libytheinae*) in one group. However, now Judies have been found to be much closer to Lycaenids (blues), while the Beaks have been found to be closely allied to the Nymphalids. Judies lay small, dome-shaped, white eggs on or near their food plants. The wood-louse shaped green caterpillar is very much like that of other Lycaenids, except that its head is visible. The caterpillar usually stays on the undersides of the leaves. For pupation, however, it invariably wanders away from the food plant. The pupa is tightly attached to the underside of a leaf, which is slightly drawn together by silk to form a protective cover. The pupa lies on a bed of whitish powder, attached to the leaf by its tail and a silken body-band. None of these butterflies is found in the Indian plains; they are confined to wooded or hilly country. In this group, the Plum Judy is the commonest.

Plum Judy

A fairly small, brown butterfly, the Plum Judy keeps to shady undergrowth until late afternoon or evening, when it can be seen chasing its own kind erratically along forest paths. It never visits flowers—overripe fruits are its favourite. It may often be seen on such fruits, probing for juices, its wings half open. In fact, its wings are so constructed that it can never close them completely. The male has a purple sheen on its brown upperside, while the female is all brown. The Plum Judy is confined to the wooded country of peninsular India up to south Gujarat, through Madhya Pradesh, Bihar, and West Bengal. In the Himalayan foothills, it is found from Chamba in Himachal Pradesh to regions further eastwards.

MILKWEED BUTTERFLIES—THE DANAIDS

This is an interesting group of butterflies that has evolved several strategies to survive. As they feed on poisonous plants such as milkweeds, oleanders, dogbanes, and figs, these butterflies are distasteful and are, therefore, usually left alone by predators who recognize them by their striking colour patterns that are advertised by their slow, sailing flight. On this 'distasteful' reputation of Danaids, other look-alike butterflies also survive even though they have no such in-built chemical defence. Milkweeds themselves contribute to such deceit and several closely related species resemble each other, reinforcing their reputation.

Besides feeding on nectar, Milkweeds are often seen clustered around dead and withered Heliotropium *and* Crotalaria *plants. The sap provides them with pyrrolizidine alkaloids, which are essential for the production of male pheromones. These alkaloids are also known to contribute towards making these butterflies unpalatable. The male possesses a pair of specialized brush-like organs, called hair pencils, which can be pushed out from the abdomen tip to disperse scent attractive to females.*

Milkweeds lay eggs singly on the upper or underside of leaves on growing shoots of the food plant. Their eggs are creamish white and barrel-shaped, flattened at the base and dome-shaped at the top, with crisscrossing longitudinal and horizontal ridges or ribs, giving an impression of minute depressions. The cylindrical, smooth caterpillar has bright colour patterns of bands and spots that serve to warn predators. In addition, it has two to four pairs of fleshy tentacles. The pupa hangs freely by its tail and has brown, golden, or silver markings.

Some of the Milkweed butterflies are the commonest butterflies found in practically every part of India. The largest among them is the Tree Nymph that occurs only in the wet forests of the Western Ghats and Sunderbans. Its wingspan can be up to 160 mm and it probably has the slowest flight of all Indian butterflies.

PLAIN TIGER (*DANAUS CHRYSIPPUS*)
WINGSPAN: 70–80 MM (PLATE 8)

This is the most familiar butterfly in Indian gardens. It is found throughout India, including in the desert region and the hills up to 9000 feet (*c.* 3000 m). Basically, it is a butterfly of the open plains where its food plant *rui* or *aak* (*Calotropis sp.*) grows in abundance. Being distasteful, it is mimicked by several species of butterflies, of which the commonest and most perfect mimic is the female Danaid Eggfly, a Nymphalid (Plate 8).

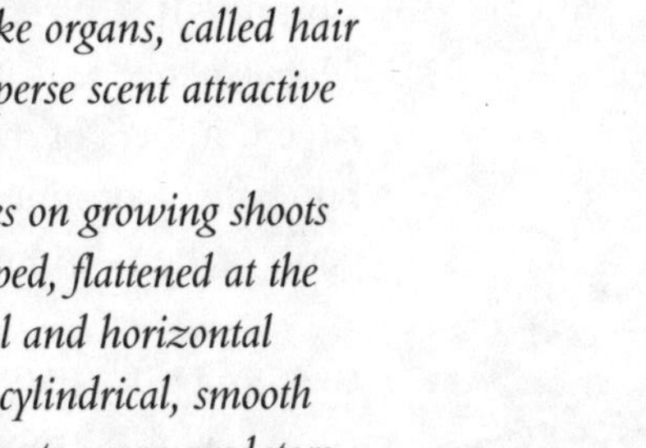

Plain Tiger

STRIPED TIGER (*DANAUS GENUTIA*)
WINGSPAN: 75–95 MM (PLATE 2)
Its rich, tawny wings with bold black stripes make this a handsome and conspicuous insect. Though it does occur almost throughout India, it is more common where rainfall is abundant and prefers forest edges and scrub jungles. In the hills, it is found up to 8000 feet (*c.* 2700 m). It has the typical slow, deliberate flight which all Milkweed butterflies use to advertise their unpalatable nature. The Striped Tiger is often seen with other Milkweed butterflies in large numbers during migratory flights.

BLUE TIGER (*TIRUMALA LIMNIACE*)
WINGSPAN: 90–100 MM (PLATE 2)

Striped Tiger

This is a common butterfly almost throughout India, both in the hills and in the plains, but not in deserts and at high altitudes. It is a frequent visitor to gardens. The Pink Cockscomb (*Ageratum conyzoides*) is its favourite flower. During the dry season, large numbers of these butterflies are often seen along with other Milkweed butterflies, roosting together in sheltered cool forests or plantations. Similar congregations are seen during their migratory flights.

GLASSY TIGER (*PARANTICA AGLEA*)
WINGSPAN: 70–85 MM (PLATE 2)

Blue Tiger

A look-alike of the Blue Tiger, it is, however, small in size with transparent markings that are whitish. Males have scent patches instead of scent pouches on the hind wings. This butterfly occurs from Mumbai southwards in peninsular India and then from Jammu eastwards up to Assam and even further. It is found in forests as well as in the open country where rainfall is heavy. Its caterpillars feed on *Tylohora carnosa*, *Cryptolephis buchanani*, and *Ceropegia sp*.

MALABAR TREE NYMPH (*IDEA MALABARICA*) WINGSPAN: 110–160 MM
It is the largest among the Milkweed butterflies and is probably the slowest flier among Indian butterflies. This butterfly is capable of hovering effortlessly at one spot, riding the air with its large semi-transparent greyish-white wings. However, when alarmed, it can make a swift escape. It is confined to the wet, evergreen forests of the Western Ghats. A closely related species, *Idea agamarschana*, occurs in the Sunderbans.

Glassy Tiger

Malabar Tree Nymph

COMMON INDIAN CROW (*EUPOLOEA CORE*)
WINGSPAN 85–95 MM (PLATE 1)

Among the Milkweed butterflies, this is the most abundantly found. A possible reason is that its caterpillars feed on a wide range of food plants including Peepal (*Ficus religiosa*), Banyan (*F. bengalensis*), and other *Ficus sp*., Oleander (*Nerium sp.*), Sandpaper tree (*Streblus asper*), and several Asclepiads. Males are often seen sailing to and fro with their abdomen curled and powder-puff-like yellow hair-pencils extended. Large congregations are seen roosting together before and during migration.

BROWNS—THE SATYRIDS

Most Browns are common and often abundant, but are seen less due to their retiring habits. They keep to shady undergrowth, where they may be seen in slow, jerky flight close to the ground. Their dull brown or blackish colour makes them quite inconspicuous as they prefer to rest among fallen leaves and stones. A marked seasonal variation is noticed among these butterflies, especially among the Evening Browns, Bushbrowns, and Rings. In the wet season, the undersides of their wings have a series of eye-like spots (ocelli), which diminish or disappear altogether in the dry season. These butterflies are not fond of flowers. Fruit, oozing tree-sap, and palm toddy are more to their taste.

Browns are mainly forest insects and lay their melon-shaped eggs singly or in clusters according to species on grasses, bamboos, and palms. The caterpillars come in shades of brown, green, yellow, and even pink, and always have two points at the tail end and two horn-like points on the head. When not feeding, the well-camouflaged caterpillars lie motionless on the undersides of leaf blades, within two or three feet of the ground, in sheltered places. The pupae hang by their tails and in some species, pupation takes place on the ground in a loosely-woven cocoon. The suspended pupae resemble those of the Milkweed butterflies, but are much more slender, with no metallic markings. Both caterpillars and pupae come under heavy attack from parasitic wasps, though the pupae can wriggle to make a dull, knocking sound.

Generally the Browns are not sun-worshippers and may be seen flying weakly even on the cloudiest day. However, a few hill dwellers, like the Meadowbrowns, Walls, and most Rings love to bask and fly in the sun.

COMMON EVENING BROWN (*MELANITIS LEDA*)
WINGSPAN: 60–80 MM (PLATE 1)

This is a familiar butterfly, very common throughout India, except in the arid northwest. It is active in the early morning and at dusk, resting in the undergrowth and among fallen leaves for most of the day. It does come to flowers but is more partial to overripe fruits and tree sap. Seasonal variation is very distinctive in this butterfly. The two-horned caterpillar feeds on rice and other grasses.

BAMBOO TREEBROWN (*LETHE EUROPA*)
WINGSPAN: 65–75 MM (PLATE 5)

Treebrowns are a large group of sombre, brown butterflies, of which some are very alike, with only minor differences. They are more forest insects and found where bamboo is common. They are active only in the mornings and evenings, and spend most of the day in bamboo clumps and undergrowth. Rotting fruits, toddy sap, fresh dung, and dead crabs are their favourite foods. The Bamboo Treebrown ranges from south India to Madhya Pradesh, Orissa, and up to Bengal. In the Himalayas, it is found from Dehra Dun to Assam and even further eastwards.

Bamboo Treebrown

COMMON TREEBROWN (*LETHE ROHRIA*)
WINGSPAN: 58–70 MM

This butterfly is at home both in the jungle and in fairly open country. It is attracted to animal dung, overripe fruits, and sugary tree sap. It is a weak flier that keeps to the ground and when disturbed, flies a little distance to settle again. It is common in peninsular India up to Madhya Pradesh and south Bihar. In the north, it ranges from Kashmir further eastwards.

COMMON BUSHBROWN (*MYCALESIS PERSEUS*)
WINGSPAN: 38–55 MM

The Bushbrowns form another large group of drab-coloured, similar looking, medium-sized butterflies. There is usually a pale line across the undersides of the wings, with a row of eye-spots at the margin. During the dry season, these markings are much reduced. Identifying and distinguishing them from one another, therefore, becomes all the more difficult.

The Common Bushbrown is a butterfly of wetter and wooded regions and keeps to shady places. When alarmed, it swiftly disappears among the bushes. Overripe fruit draw this butterfly out. It is found in most parts of India.

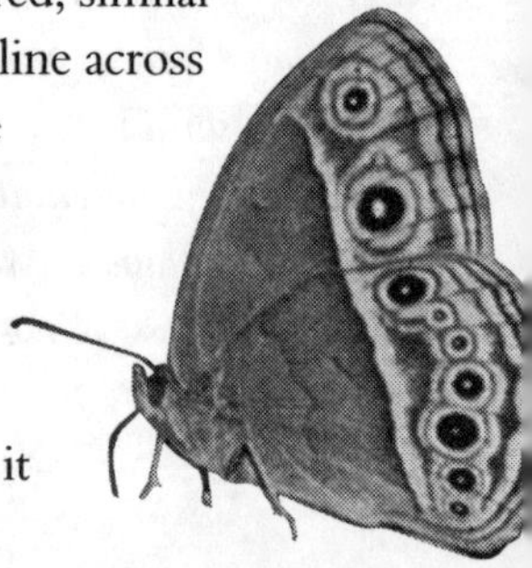

Dark Brand Bushbrowns

Gladeye Bushbrown

DARK BRAND BUSHBROWNS (*MYCALESIS MINEUS*)
WINGSPAN: 40–50 MM (PLATE 5)
This butterfly occurs in peninsular India up to Madhya Pradesh, Orissa, and Bengal. In the Himalayas, it is seen from Kullu further eastwards. It keeps to undergrowth and is common in the wetter parts of India. Its double-horned caterpillar feeds on grasses and often wanders off to pupate on other plants.

GLADEYE BUSHBROWN (*MYCALESIS PATNIA*) WINGSPAN: 40–45 MM
The large, comical, eye-like markings on the underside of this butterfly are unmistakable. It dwells in the evergreen and bamboo forests of peninsular India and to the south of Maharashtra, where it can be seen flying weakly along paths. Overripe fruits, toddy, and other sugary tree saps are its favourite foods.

Nigger

NIGGER (*ORSOTRIAENA MEDUS*) WINGSPAN: 45–55 MM (PLATE 5)
This feeble flier always keeps close to the shady forest floor. It is widely distributed in south India in regions suited to its habits, and from Sikkim further eastwards. The straight white band across its wings on the underside is unmistakable.

Common Fourring

COMMON FOURRING (*YPTHIMA HUEBNERI*)
WINGSPAN: 30–40 MM
The group of small butterflies known as Rings gets its name from the bold eye-spots or rings that mark the underside of the hind wings. The number and location of such markings vary between species and are a tool for their identification. These markings are seasonal and almost disappear during dry periods.

The Common Fourring, a small, greyish-brown butterfly, is at home in the open plains as well as in forests and in the hills. It is seen up to 5000 feet (*c.* 1700 m) and is one of the commonest butterflies found throughout India. It is much weaker on its wings than the Common Fivering.

Common Fivering

COMMON FIVERING (*YPTHIMA BALDUS*)
WINGSPAN: 32–48 MM (PLATE 5)
This is one of the most abundantly seen butterflies, occurring almost all over India. When disturbed, it flies with typical jerky movements, only to settle again nearby. Fond of flowers, it can often be seen basking in the sun with its wings three-fourths open.

BRUSH-FOOTED BUTTERFLIES—THE NYMPHALIDS

The Nymphalids are a large group of robust-bodied butterflies that come in almost every shape and colour. Some of them are strikingly handsome, with the undersides of their wings generally drab and cryptically coloured. The majority of them are strong fliers and love to bask in the sun. Males of this group are particularly quarrelsome and can be seen policing their territory. Some do visit flowers but they are generally more partial to overripe fruits, tree sap, and even animal dung and urine. Butterflies like the Tawny Rajah and Nawabs do not visit flowers at all. Mudpuddling is not very popular with this group, but some species are frequently found on damp spots.

As with the adults, in the early stages, Nymphalids too vary in form and colour. Nymphalid eggs may be dome-shaped or spherical, ribbed, pitted, knobbed, or smooth, and are laid singly or in clusters. Caterpillars are cylindrical, some with fleshy or hairy spines, others smooth with horns on the head. Pupae hang freely by their tails and have angular projections. Some have metallic golden or silver markings on the projections. However, the pupae of the Tawny Rajah and Nawabs are smooth, without any metallic markings.

The first pair of legs in these butterflies have brush-like dense tufts, but being imperfectly developed and clawless, these legs are not used for perching or walking. Hence Nymphalids appear to have only four legs. They share this particular characteristic with the Browns and the Milkweed butterflies. Modern taxonomists have classified the Browns and the Milkweed butterflies as subfamilies of the Nymphalidae family.

The family Nymphalidae has been recently re-classified, with the result that several groups of butterflies that were thought to be distinct families are now included as subfamilies of Nymphalidae. Disagreement among taxonomists regarding the exact status of these subfamilies still continues.

Earlier, Amathusids were also considered to be a separate family. But now, according to some taxonomists, they are just a subfamily of the Nymphalidae. These uncommon butterflies are not only closely related to the Browns but their food plants and habits too are similar. Only the Southern Duffer is found in the forests of South India, while the rest of this group are confined to the thick jungles of the Northeast, so we will not describe these butterflies here.

JOKER (*BYBLIA ILITHYIA*) WINGSPAN: 45–55 MM (PLATE 6)

An inhabitant of dry, open, grassy plains, this butterfly ranges throughout the drier parts of peninsular India and further north up to Madhya Pradesh and Kutchch in the west. It is more an African butterfly that is found in dry regions of that continent. Surprisingly, in spite of such wide distribution, there is no geographical subspeciation or variation in this butterfly. Its flight range is extremely limited, usually around hedges where the food plant *Tragia cannabina* grows.

Joker

ANGLED CASTOR (*ARIADNE ARIADNE*) WINGSPAN: 45–60 MM (PLATE 6)

Angled Castor

Both this butterfly and its close cousin, the Common Castor (*A. merione*), have similar distribution throughout India except in the arid north and northwest. They also share the same food plants. Castors are partial to overripe fruits and tree sap. The wing edges of the Common Castor are rounded and the black lines are more wavy than in the Angled Castor. The well-camouflaged caterpillars always remain on the undersides of leaves.

LEOPARD (*PHALANTA PHALANTHA*) WINGSPAN: 50–60 MM (PLATE 6)

An extremely active butterfly, the Leopard is usually seen flitting from flower to flower, with half-open wings. It occupies prominent positions in the sunlight from where it makes sorties to chase away passing butterflies. During summer, it may be seen in the mixed company of other butterflies mudpuddling on damp patches. In the plains, it lays eggs on *Flacourita spp*., and on the hills it prefers Willow (*Salix sp.*).

INDIAN FRITILLARY (*AGRYREUS HYPERBIUS*)
WINGSPAN: 65–85 MM (PLATE 6)

This is a common flier in the hills of southern, western, and central India. It ranges all along the Himalayas and in the Northeastern hills. It is sometimes seen in the plains, possibly as a winter migrant. The female mimics the Plain Tiger whom it resembles in the colour pattern of the upperside of its wings. In the south, it is on wing throughout the year, always above 6000 feet (*c.* 2000 m), while in the north, it is seen between 2000 and 9000 feet

Indian Fritillary

(*c.* 700–3000 m) from April to October. Its known food plants are a species of violets (*Viola spp.*).

TAMIL LACEWING (*CETHOSIA NIETNERI*) WINGSPAN: 80–95 MM

This beautiful tawny red butterfly is restricted to the thick jungles of South India where the rainfall is heavy. The deeply scalloped border of its hindwings and the V-shaped markings all along the wing borders are unmistakable. While on the wing, this butterfly can be mistaken for a Plain or Striped Tiger and, like several distasteful butterflies, it feigns death when attacked.

Tamil Lacewing

BLUE PANSY (*JUNONIA ORITHYA*) WINGSPAN: 40–60 MM (PLATE 6)

This is undoubtedly one of the prettiest of Indian butterflies. It is seen commonly throughout the Indian subcontinent, but is more at home in dry, open plains than in forests. It is most active during the hottest part of the day, and dry river beds and stony paths are its favourite haunts. In the plains, it flies all through the year but at higher elevations, it is found only from April to October.

Blue Pansy

YELLOW PANSY (*JUNONIA HIERTA*)
WINGSPAN: 45–60 MM (PLATE 6)

This butterfly is as pretty as its relation, the Blue Pansy, with a brilliant blue oval patch in the basal area of the bright yellow upperside of its hind wings. The habits and distribution of these two Pansies are identical. As with all Pansies, the male Yellow Pansy too is territorial and can be seen pugnaciously chasing its own kind. Fond of flowers, its favourite among garden flowers is marigold.

LEMON PANSY (*JUNONIA LEMONIAS*)
WINGSPAN: 45–60 MM

This is the commonest of the six Pansies. Like the Chocolate Pansy, it is more frequent in forests and is distributed throughout South and Central India, up to south Gujarat in the west, and West Bengal in the east. In the Himalayas, it is seen up to 8000 feet (*c.* 2700 m) from Kashmir through Assam, and even further eastwards. It is very fond of flowers and can be seen basking on the ground or on low foliage.

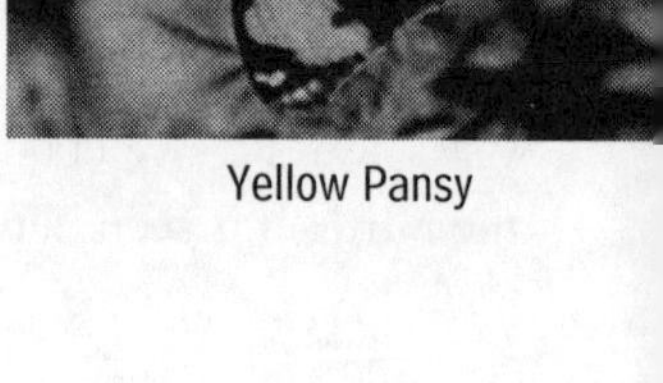

Yellow Pansy

PEACOCK PANSY (*JUNONIA ALMANA*)
WINGSPAN: 60–65 MM (PLATE 7)
Another very common Pansy, this tawny butterfly occurs throughout India. Two large eye-spots on the uppersides of its hind wings and two smaller ones on each of its fore wings make it unmistakable. The undersides too have eyespots during the wet season. During the dry season, however, the undersides resemble a leaf. This butterfly is attracted to marigold flowers.

Peacock Pansy

GREY PANSY (*JUNONIA ATLITES*) WINGSPAN: 55–65 MM
Commonly occurring only in the rain-fed, open regions of peninsular India and along the foothills of the Himalayas from Kalka in Himachal Pradesh further eastwards, this butterfly is fond of flowers. Marigolds never fail to attract Grey Pansies. At times, several of them can be seen in flocks.

CHOCOLATE PANSY (*JUNONIA IPHITA*)
WINGSPAN: 55–80 MM
It is a butterfly commonly found in the forests of South and Central India. It is also seen throughout the Himalayas up to 9000 feet (*c.* 3000 m), from Kashmir further eastwards. It is rare in the plains and absent in dry regions. It comes to flowers and may be seen on damp patches. Unlike other Pansies, this dark butterfly is more often seen in shady places.

Painted Lady

PAINTED LADY (*VANESSA CARDUI*)
WINGSPAN: 55–70 MM (PLATE 6)
This is the world's best known and most widely distributed butterfly. It is found all over the world except in South America. In India, it flies everywhere, from sea-level up to 15,000 feet (*c.* 5000 m) in the Himalayas. Being an acclaimed migrant, large numbers of these butterflies have been seen moving in swarms. The Painted Lady is more commonly met with in open places where it can be seen chasing other butterflies.

Indian Tortoiseshell

INDIAN TORTOISESHELL (*NYMPHALIS [AGLAIS] KASCH MIRENSIS*) WINGSPAN: 55–65 MM (PLATE 7)
This is the commonest Himalayan butterfly and can be seen throughout the year, even when it snows. Males are

Male and Female Danaid Eggfly

territorial and they spend much of their time basking or chasing away other butterflies.

DANAID EGGFLY (*HYPOLIMNAS MISIPPUS*)
WINGSPAN: 70–85 MM (PLATE 7)

The female of this butterfly (Plate 8) is an excellent mimic of the Plain Tiger and is less seen than her handsomely-marked male counterpart. The Danaid Eggfly prefers open country with moderate rainfall and is most abundant during the rains. The male is highly territorial and takes up prominent positions to bask, from where it chases away butterflies that pass by. Purslane or Office-time (*Portulaca spp.*) is its preferred food plant.

GREAT EGGFLY (*HYPOLIMNAS BOLINA*) WINGSPAN: 70–110 MM

The iridescent, bluish-white, egg-shaped markings on the upper wing surface make the male of this species a handsome insect. The male is highly territorial and patrols to and fro, chasing away any butterfly that comes into his territory. The female is an almost perfect mimic of the distasteful Milkweed butterfly, the Common Crow. However, on closer inspection, the two blue spots on her fore wings and broad pale yellow or white scalloped border on her hind wings give her away. This butterfly is common throughout India but is abundant in moist, well-forested country.

BLUE OAKLEAF (*KALLIMA HORSFIELDI*) WINGSPAN: 85–110 MM (PLATE 7)

This leaf-shaped butterfly is a classic example of protective resemblance and to enhance this effect, it always settles in head-down position so as to connect its rear end, that is the stalk, to the branch of the stem. This is an insect of the well-forested regions of South India where rainfall is heavy. Its close cousin, the Orange Oakleaf, is found in the Himalayas from Kashmir to Assam and eastwards, and in south Bihar, the Eastern Ghats, and the hills of Madhya Pradesh and Maharashtra. Overripe or rotting fruits are its favourite foods.

Blue Oakleaf

COMMON MAP (*CYRESTIS THYODAMAS*)
WINGSPAN: 50–60 MM (PLATE 7)

This butterfly is confined to the moist hilly forests of the Himalayas up to 8000 feet (*c.* 2700 m) and the cool moist forests of the Western Ghats. It visits flowers as well as damp patches. The map-like markings and the slow, sailing, and jerky flight make it easy to identify this fragile butterfly. Its caterpillars feed on Peepal, Banyan, and other fig species. In the Himalayas, it flies from May to October and elsewhere, all through the year.

Common Map Butterfly

CHESTNUT STREAKED SAILOR (*NEPTIS JUMBAH*)
WINGSPAN: 60–70 MM

Although this butterfly occurs throughout peninsular India, it is not as common as the ubiquitous Common Sailor. In the Himalayas, it ranges from Sikkim eastwards. It is essentially a forest insect and is a stronger flier than the Common Sailor. The Red Silk Cotton seems to be its favourite food plant.

COMMON SAILOR (*NEPTIS HYLAS*) WINGSPAN: 50–60 MM

Among the several species of Sailors found in India, this is the one most frequently encountered—almost everywhere, except in the arid north and northwest. All species of Sailors have three characteristic horizontal bands on their wings. There is no band on the body as the Sergeants have at the junction of the thorax and abdomen. A Sailor's flight is typical, as its name suggests, sailing with the wings held almost horizontal, with occasional flicks of the wings.

Chestnut Streaked Sailor

Common Sailor

COMMON SERGEANT (*ATHYMA PERIUS*)
WINGSPAN: 60–70 MM

Sergeants and Sailors are closely related butterflies. Therefore, they look alike, except that Sergeants have a white or tawny yellow band on the abdomen, which distinguishes them from Sailors. Sergeants are at home in well-wooded country where the rainfall is heavy and are often found in the hills at low and moderate heights. The Common Sergeant is fairly well-distributed in peninsular India and also in the Himalayas from Simla eastwards, including the hills of Northeast India.

COMMANDER (*MODUZA PROCRIS*) WINGSPAN: 60–75 MM

Like its close cousins, the Sergeant and Sailor, this butterfly is seen sailing gracefully with its wings held horizontally, or basking with its wings spread flat. It is more a forest insect found both in the dry and wet regions of peninsular India up to Madhya Pradesh, and from Dehra Dun to West Bengal and eastwards. Its caterpillar feed on *Mussanda sp.*

Commander

Common Sergeant

POPINJAY (*STIBOCHIONA NICEA*) WINGSPAN: 60–80 MM
This Himalayan butterfly flies from Kullu to Assam and even further eastwards up to 4000 feet (*c.* 1300 m). It is on the wing from March to October. While the males have velvet black wings with blue borders, the females are dark green with lighter green-bordered wings. They are often seen on damp spots with their wings spread flat.

COMMON BARON (*EUTHALIA ACONTHEA*) WINGSPAN: 55–80 MM (PLATE 1)
The Common Baron is a frequent visitor to gardens, but instead of flowers, it chooses to settle on a damp patch, using its proboscis to gather moisture. Rotten fruits and oozing tree sap also attract this butterfly. It is a strong flier that ranges throughout India up to 4000 feet (*c.* 1300 m) in the hills. Its caterpillar presents a remarkable example of effective camouflage while it rests along the mid-vein of a mango leaf.

Baronet

BARONET OR RED BARON (*EUTHALIA NAIS*)
WINGSPAN: 60–70 MM (PLATE 7)
This bright, tawny orange butterfly is a familiar sight on forest roads. If disturbed, it flies off only to settle again a short distance away. It prefers drier forests and is attracted by sweet tree sap and rotten fruits. It occurs in peninsular India and northwards up to south Gujarat in the west, up to Dehra Dun in the north, and up to Sikkim in the east. Its caterpillar is very similar to the Baron's and feeds on Ebony or *tendu* and *sal*.

BLACK PRINCE (*ROHANA PARISATIS*)
WINGSPAN: 45–50 MM
The male is velvet black except for two white dots at the wing-tips and the female is very much like the Castor butterfly. In flight too, the male and the female differ: the male is swift while the the female is slow and lazy. Confined to the hilly forests of South India, in the north, it is seen from Kumaon further eastwards.

Common Nawab

COMMON NAWAB (*POLYURA ATHAMAS*)
WINGSPAN: 60–75 MM (PLATE 7)
This is a fast flier that occurs in peninsular India up to south Gujarat and Madhya Pradesh. In the north, it flies from Kullu eastwards through Assam and even further east.

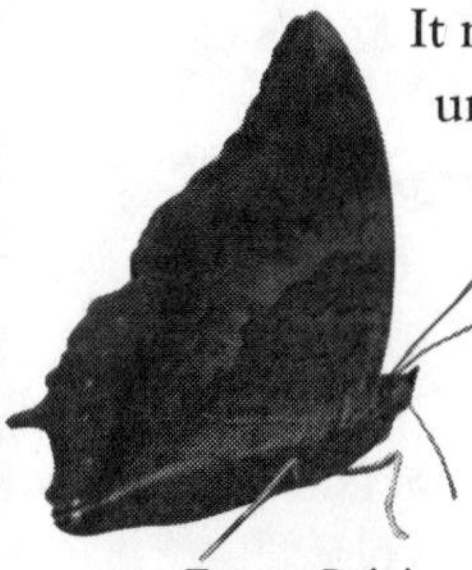

Tawny Rajah

It never visits flowers—a day-old dead crab, animal dung, or urine are more to its taste. Greenish-yellow bands on the dark green body perfectly camouflage the four-horned caterpillar among small-leaved leguminous trees like *Acacia* and *Caesalpinia*.

TAWNY RAJAH (*CHARAXES BERNARDUS*) WINGSPAN: 90–100 MM (PLATE 7)

This butterfly is one of the most powerful fliers: it has been recorded to fly at sixty kilometres per hour and even more. It is found in the forests of peninsular India, Madhya Pradesh, Bihar, Orissa, and also in the Himalayas from Mussoorie eastwards. Flowers do not attract this butterfly, but dead crabs, animal dung, urine, toddy saps, and overripe fruits do. It is often seen on damp patches during the pre and post-monsoon periods.

Black Rajah

BLACK RAJAH (*CHARAXES SOLON*) WINGSPAN: 70–80 MM

Although widely distributed throughout India except in the northwest, this dark brown butterfly is not so common. The tails at the hind wings are longer in the females and more pointed in the males. The Black Rajah is more likely to be found in drier plains and its favourite food plant is Tamarind. Overripe fruits, toddy sap, and animal dung and urine are other attractions.

Tawny Coster

TAWNY COSTER (*ACRAEA TERPSICORE*) WINGSPAN: 50–65 MM (PLATE 7)

Birds and lizards ignore this slow-flying butterfly, for even the slightest touch brings forth an oily, smelly liquid from the glands situated in its body joints. Common throughout India, it is a frequent visitor to gardens where it can be seen fluttering from flower to flower. Its yellow, dome-shaped eggs are laid in clusters on the creepers of Passion Flowers (*Passiflora spp.*) and Cucumbers (*Cucurbitacae spp.*).

Yellow Coster

YELLOW COSTER (*ACRAEA ISSORIA*) WINGSPAN: 45–85 MM

This is a yellowish-brown butterfly that occurs in the Himalayas between 2000 and 7000 feet (*c.* 700–2300 m) from Kullu further eastwards. It is at home in open scrub areas where it can be seen in slow, fluttering flight. Like the Tawny Coster, it lays eggs in clusters. Its spiny, black caterpillars live together on *Boehmeria* or *Buddlieia* plants.

Common Beak

COMMON BEAK (*LIBYTHEA CELTIS*)
WINGSPAN: 45–50 MM

The extraordinary long, beak-like palpi give this butterfly its name. Its wings too have a typical shape. Basically a hill dweller, this butterfly occurs in the hills of South India. In the north, it flies from Kashmir further eastwards, all along the Himalayas, between 3000 and 9000 feet (*c.* 1000– 3000 m). It never visits flowers but may be seen on damp patches.

SKIPPERS—THE HESPERIIDS

Their fast, darting flight, which is quite distinct from that of other butterflies, gives this group of butterflies their popular name. Structurally, the robust-bodied Skippers are said to be primitive, much like moths. They are often seen basking with their fore wings folded flat on either side of their bodies. Their antennae are thickly clubbed, with tapering, curved or hooked tips.

Skippers lay their eggs singly on the upper or underside of a leaf, or at its tip. The large, dome-shaped eggs have ridges, running from top to bottom, and may be red or white in colour. The caterpillar binds a leaf with silk to make a cell for itself from which it emerges to feed, usually at night. The majority of Skippers feed on grasses, palms, bamboos, and gingers. The pupa is also enclosed within the leaf. In some species, the pupa is covered with white powder, possibly to repel moisture.

Basically, Skippers are forest insects, though some may be found on open plains, especially in grassy meadows. The majority of Skippers are found in the hills of the Northeast. A lot of them are active just after sunrise and some, in the evenings. The Golden Angle is known to fly at night as well.

COMMON BANDED AWL (*HASORA CHROMUS*)
WINGSPAN: 45–50 MM (PLATE 5)

This large Skipper is common throughout India, both in the forests and in open country. Its flight is extremely rapid and bounding. It is active during the early part of the day, when it may be seen on flowers, and by midday, it retires beneath

Common Banded Awl

leaves. The caterpillars roll Pongam leaves into cells within which they stay and feed. Pupation takes place within the leaf shelter.

Brown Awl

BROWN AWL (*BADAMIA EXCLAMATIONIS*)
WINGSPAN: 50–55 MM (PLATE 5)
This long-winged, large Skipper occurs throughout India and is more common in the wooded areas. A strong flier, with a rapid, bounding flight, it is attracted to flowers and bird-droppings. *Terminalia belerica* is its favourite food plant, on which its brightly banded caterpillars can be seen.

Malabar Spotted Flat

MALABAR SPOTTED FLAT
(*CELAENORRHINUS AMBAREESA*)
WINGSPAN: 45–55 MM (PLATE 5)
This is a butterfly of the shady forests of peninsular India, also found in the southern parts of the Indo-Gangetic plain. The male can be seen policing his territory in the mornings. This species could be mistaken for other Flats, especially the Tamil Spotted Flat and the Common Spotted Flat, but for the prominent chequered fringe around the fore and hind wings. Its antennae, too, are chequered and have white bands below the clubs.

Golden Angle

GOLDEN ANGLE (*CAPRONA RANSONNETTI*)
WINGSPAN: 35–45 MM (PLATE 5)
This is one of the Flats which, unlike typical Skippers, rests with its wings spread across the surface on which it sits. Males are highly territorial and fights between them are frequent. They may be seen perched along forest paths displaying their hair pencils, which give them a bearded appearance. They are found in the jungles of South India, extending up to the Pachmarhi Hills in Central India, through Orissa, south Bihar, and Assam eastwards. Its hair-crested caterpillar makes shelters of *Helicteres* and *Triamphata* leaves and also feeds on them.

GRASS DEMON (*UDASPES FOLUS*) WINGSPAN: 40–48 MM (PLATE 5)
Large, semi-transparent, white spots on the fore wings and the conspicuous semi-transparent, white, central areas on the hind wings are very distinctive features of this Skipper. It is found throughout South India, extending up to

Grass Demon

the Saurashtra region of Gujarat, through Madhya Pradesh to Uttar Pradesh, and from Kangra eastwards, including West Bengal. Caterpillars roll ginger and turmeric leaves into shelters and also feed on them. Pupation is within the leaf shelter.

COMMON REDEYE (*MATAPA ARIA*)
WINGSPAN: 40–45 MM (PLATE 5)

This native of bamboo jungles is easily distinguishable from most other Skippers by its red eyes. Its big cousin, the Giant Redeye, is much larger (70–76 mm) and occurs mainly in hill forests. An early flier, the Common Redeye can be seen basking in the morning sun. It is widely distributed throughout South India, and in the north, it is found from Dehra Dun further eastwards.

Common Redeye

DARK PALM DART (*TELICOTA BAMBUSAE*)
WINGSPAN: 34–36 MM (PLATE 5)

This butterfly is common throughout India except in the arid northwest. It is more a denizen of the jungle where its food plant, bamboo, is available. It is a fast flier that settles on flowers and on bird-droppings, wetting them with liquid that it sprays from its body by curling its abdomen. It prefers shade, but also basks with its fore wings held slightly apart and hind wings almost flat on the surface where it rests.

Dark Palm Dart

CONJOINED SWIFT
(*PELOPIDAS CONJUNCTA*)
WINGSPAN: 45–52 MM (PLATE 5)

This large Skipper is seen mainly during the monsoon and a couple of months after, when its food plant, wild *sorhgum* (a tall grass with white, bead-like, hard seeds), grows in abundance. Its range covers peninsular India as well as the north from Dehra Dun eastwards.

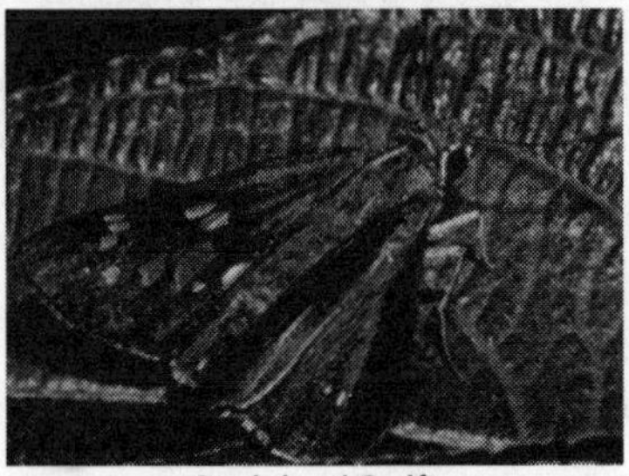

Conjoined Swift

PREFERRED LARVAL FOOD PLANTS OF SOME BUTTERFLIES

BUTTERFLY	FOOD PLANTS
SWALLOWTAILS	
Southern Birdwing	Indian Birthwort (*Aristolochia indica*), *Thottea wallichi*, and garden varieties of Birthwort
Common Rose	Indian Birthwort (*A. indica*), Calico Flower (*A. elegans*) and other garden varieties of Birthwort
Crimson Rose	Indian Birthwort (*Aristolochia indica*)
Common Mime	Cinnamon (*Cinnamomum zeylanicum*), Laurels (*Litsea chinensis*, *L. sebifera*)
Lime Butterfly and Common Mormon	Cultivated lime and oranges, *ban nimbu* (*Glycosmis pentaphylla*), *bael* (*Aegle marmelos*), Curry-leaf plant or *kadipatta* (*Murraya koenigi*)
Blue Mormon	*Ban nimbu* (*Glycosmis pentaphylla*) and other varieties of wild and cultivated lime and oranges
Common Bluebottle	Cinnamon, Laurels (*Machilus* sp.)
Tailed Jay	Custard Apple or *sitaphal* (*Anona squamosa*), False Ashok or Mast Tree (*Polyalthia longifolia*), *Miliusa tomentosa*, *champak* (*Michelia champaca*)
Spot Swordtail	*Polyalthia cerasoides*, *Miliusa tomentosa*

BUTTERFLY	FOOD PLANTS
WHITES AND YELLOWS	
Common Jezebel	Mistletoe (*Dendrophthoe* sp.)
Psyche	Caper (*Capparis heyneana*), Sacred Barna (*Crataeva religiosa*)
Indian Cabbage White	Cultivated cabbage
Common Gull	Capers (*Capparis* spp.)
Pioneer	Capers
Small Salmon Arab	Salt Bush (*Salvodora persica*)
White Orange Tip	Capers
Yellow Orange Tip	Capers
Great Orange Tip	Sacred Barna, Capers
Common Wanderer	Capers
Common Emigrant	*Amaltas* or Indian Laburnum (*Cassia fistula*), Siamese Cassia (*Cassia siamea*) and other *Cassia spp*., Flame of the Forest or *palas* (*Butea monosperma*), *Bauhinia racemosa*
Mottled Emigrant	*Cassia tora*, *C. auriculata*, *C. occidentalis*
Common Grass Yellow	Amaltas (*Cassia fistula*), English Tamarind (*Pithecellobium dulce*), *sirish* (*Albizzia* sp.), *Sesbania aculeata*, *Caesalpinia spp*.
BLUES	
Common Pierrot (larva attended by ants intermittently)	Indian Jujube or *ber* (*Zizyphus spp*.)

BUTTERFLY	FOOD PLANTS
Angled Pierrot (larva attended by ants intermittently)	*Zizyphus rugosa*
Zebra Blue (larva attended by ants intermittently)	Buds of sirish (*Albizzia lebbeck*), *Indigofera spp.*, *Sesbania spp.*, *chitrak* (*Plumbago spp.*)
Pale Grass Blue (larva attended by ants intermittently)	*Oxalis corniculata*, *Tephrosia sp.*, *Nelsonia sp.*, *karvi*
Lime Blue (larva attended by ants intermittently)	Orange, lime and related *Citrus spp.*
Grass Jewel (larva attended by ants intermittently)	Pea pods, *Heliotropium sp.*, Indigo
Gram Blue (larva attended by ants intermittently)	Flame of Forest, *Acacia spp.*, and pods of cultivated peas, beans, and gram
Pea Blue (larva attended by ants intermittently)	Flame of the Forest and pods of cultivated peas, gram, and beans
Common Cerulean (larva attended by ants intermittently)	Flowers and leaves of *karanj*, Crab-eyed creeper (*Abrus precatorius*), Ashok (*Saraca asoca*), Flame of the Forest or palas
Red Pierrot	*Bryophyllum spp.*, *Kalanchoe spp.*
Large Oakblue (larva attended by ants constantly)	*Ain* (*Terminalia tomentosa*), Indian Almond (*T. catappa*), Queen's Flower or *jarool* (*Lagerstromia speciosa*)
Common Acacia Blue (larva attended by ants constantly)	*Acacia sp.*
Leaf Blue	*Olax sp.*
Common Silverline (larva attended by ants constantly)	Bitter Hedge Plant (*Clerodendrum inerme*), Ber (*Zizyphus spp.*)

BUTTERFLY	FOOD PLANTS
Yamfly (larva attended by ants constantly)	Yam (*Dioscorea pentaphylla*), *Smilax sp.*
Monkey Puzzle	*Ixora spp.*, Mistletoe (*Dendrophthoe sp.*), *kusum* (*Schleichera oleosa*), *kumbhi* (*Careya arborea*), *Eugenia zeylanica*
Cornelian	Inside fruits like pomegranate, wood apple (*Limonia acidissima*), *ghela* (*Randia sp.*)
Indian Red Flash (larva attended by ants constantly)	Flowers of *Ougenia dalbergioides*, ber or Indian Jujube
Indian Sunbeam	Karanj, Crab-eyed creeper, *Derris scandens*, *Xylia sp.*
Plum Judy	*Embelia robusta*, *Ardisia sp.*
MILKWEED BUTTERFLIES	
Plain Tiger	*Rui* or *aak* (*Calotropis procera* and *C. gigantea*)
Striped Tiger	*Ceropegia aculata*, *C. intermedia*, *Cynanchum dalhousie*, *Raphistemma pulchellum*
Blue Tiger	Blood flower (*Asclepias curasavica*), *chiti* (*Marsdenia tenacissima*), Wax plant (*Hoya sp.*), *Wattaakaka volubilis*
Glassy Tiger	*Tylophora carnosa*, *Cryptolepis buchanani*, and *Ceropegia sp.*
Malabar Tree Nymph	*Aganosma cymosa*
Common Indian Crow	Oleander (*Nerium oleander* and *N. indicum*), *kuda* or *kurchi* (*Holarrhena pubescens*), *kalidudhi* or *krishnawara* (*Ichnocarpus frutescens*), Banyan (*Ficus bengalensis*), Peepal (*Ficus religiosa*), *umbar* or *gular* (*F. racemosa*), Indian

BUTTERFLY	FOOD PLANTS
	Rubber (*F. elastica*), Sand Paper Tree (*Streblus asper*), *anantvel* or *nannari* (*Hemidesmus indicus*), *Cryptolepis buchanani*
BROWNS	
Common Evening Brown	Rice (*Oryza sativa*), *Hetropogon contortus*, and other grasses
Bamboo Treebrown	Bamboo
Common Treebrown	Bamboo
Common Bushbrown	Grasses
Dark Brand Bushbrown	Grasses
Gladeye Bushbrown	Grasses
Nigger	Grasses
Common Fourring	Grasses
Common Fivering	Grasses
NYMPHALIDS	
Joker	*Tragia cannabina*
Common Castor and Angled Castor	Castor oil plant (*Rivinus communis*), *Tragia sp.*
Leopard	*Flacourtia montana*, *F. ramontchii*
Indian Fritillary	Violets (*Viola sp.*)
Tamil Lacewing	Wild and cultivated Passion Flowers
Blue Pansy	*Justicia procumbens*, *J. migrantha*, *Lepidagathis prostrata*

BUTTERFLY	FOOD PLANTS
Yellow Pansy	*Talimkhana* (*Hygrophila auriculata*),*Barleria sp.*
Lemon Pansy	Talimkhana, Jute (*Corchorus olitorious*), *Lepidagathis sp.*, *Nelsonia canescens*
Peacock Pansy	Talimkhana, *Barleria sp.*, *Osbeckia sp.*
Grey Pansy	Talimkhana, *Barleria sp.*
Chocolate Pansy	Karvi, *Justicia sp.*, Talimkhana.
Painted Lady	*Zorina diphylla*, *Artemisia sp.*, Blumea, Nettles (*Urtica sp.*)
Indian Tortoiseshell	*Bichhu*-grass or Nettles (*Urtica sp.*)
Danaid Eggfly	Purslane (*Portulaca oleracea*), *Abutilon sp.*
Great Eggfly	Purslane (*Portulaca oleracea*), *Fleurya interrupta*, *Elatostemma cunneatum*
Blue Oakleaf	Karvi (*Carvia callosa*), *Strobilanthes sp.*
Common Map	Peepal (*Ficus religiosa*), Banyan (*F. bengalensis*), umber or gular (*F. racemosa*)
Chestnut Streaked Sailor	Karanj (*Pongamia pinnata*), *shisham*, Red Silk Cotton, *bhendi* or Portia Tree (*Thespesia populnea*), *Wagatea spicata*, *Grewia sp.*
Common Sailor	Red Silk Cotton, East-Indian Screw Tree (*Helicteres isora*), *Grewia sp.*, *Mucuna sp.*
Common Sergeant	*Glochidion sp.*
Commander	Cinchona, *Mussanda frondosa*, *kadam* (*Anthocephalus cadamba*), *kalam* (*Mitragyna parvifolia*)
Common Baron	Mango (*Mangifera idica*), Cashew (*Anacardium occidentale*)

BUTTERFLY	**FOOD PLANTS**
Baronet	Ebony or *tendu* (*Diosphyros melanoxylon*), *sal* (*Shorea robust*)
Black Prince	*Celtis tetrandra*, *C. lycodoxylon*
Common Nawab	*Khair* (*Acacia catechu*), sirish (*Albizzia lebbeck*), *gulmohur* (*Delonix regia*), Coralwood or *ratan gunj* (*Adenanthera pavonia*), Sappan Wood (*Ceasalpinia sappan*), Fever-Nut (*C. bonducella*)
Tawny Rajah	*Miliusa tomentosa*, Tamarind (*Tamarindus indicus*)
Black Rajah	Tamarind, *Wagatea spicata*
Tawny Coster	Cultivated Passion Flowers and *Modecca palmata*, *Passiflora foetida*
Yellow Coster	*Boehmeria sp.*, *Debregasia sp.*, *Buddelia sp.*
Common Beak	*Celtis australis*
SKIPPERS	
Common Banded Awl	Karanj or Pongam (*Pongamia pinnata*), Castor Oil Plant (*Ricinus communis*)
Brown Awl	*Terminalis belirica*
Malabar Spotted Flat	Karvi (*Carvia allosa*), *Strobilanthes sp.*
Golden Angle	Indian Screw Tree (*Helicteres isora*), *Triumfetta rhomboidea*
Grass Demon	Wild Turmeric (*Curcuma spp.*) Ginger Lily (*Hedychium spp.*)
Common Redeye	Bamboo
Dark Palm Dart	Bamboo
Conjoined Swift	Bamboo, *Sorghum halepensa*

VARIATION

Variation within species of butterflies is quite common, occurring in size, shape, and colour, and also behavioural patterns. These variations are attributable to both genetic and non-genetic factors. Genetic variability is found in specimens of the same group, creating diverse individuals. Offsprings differ from each other, despite their common origin and fundamental heredity, mainly due to changes in the genetic make-up during the course of development and evolutionary processes. Environmental factors such as geography, climate, season, etc. have also made an impact. They influence the distribution, movement, and life-cycle of butterflies, resulting in different forms. Four major types of variability, namely individual variability, sexual dimorphism, seasonal variability, and geographical variability are found among butterflies.

India, being a vast country, with wide contrasts in physical features, climate, and vegetation, possesses one of the richest and most varied butterfly fauna in the world. These same factors cause some minor but well-marked differences in size, coloration, and other features among butterflies of the same kind distributed throughout India. A butterfly from the north of India will differ slightly from the same species in the south. Often, such geographical variations give rise to races or subspecies. The Painted Lady is an exception and does not show any such variation because being a strong migrant, there are no isolated populations of this butterfly that may develop their own unique features. Prolonged isolation, such as on oceanic islands, usually cause races to evolve into separate species.

Individual variation is also common in some butterflies: for example, the undersides of two Oakleaf butterflies seldom match. Between sexes too, there is variation, owing to which the male and the female differ from each other in detail, though they otherwise resemble each other to a considerable extent. Female Danaid and Great Eggflies are, however, so different from their males that it is difficult to believe that they are of the same species. The female Common Mormon occurs in three forms, whereas in the Common Mime, both sexes occur in two forms to mimic the Common Crow and Blue Tiger. Some butterflies show seasonal variations through two forms—the dry season form (DSF) and the wet season form (WSF). The Common Evening Brown has a series of eyespots on the wing border during the monsoon, while in the summer, it is almost invisible among the leaves due its mottled brown colour. The Bushbrowns too have such seasonal forms. The undersides of the Peacock Pansy lose their eyespots and become paler in the DSF, and additionally, its wings assume a leaf-like shape.

PROTECTIVE ADAPTATIONS

Butterflies at all stages face the prospect of attack by predators. To escape from their enemies and to protect themselves, butterflies have developed various protective devices, which are used right from the caterpillar stage. Most caterpillars come in shades of green and brown, which camouflage them among their food plants. The effect is further enhanced by their being marked with lines very much like the veins of a leaf, or by lateral lines that optically break up their body pattern among the blades of grass.

Caterpillars of Skippers roll leaves around themselves to remain concealed. Leaf-mining caterpillars of the Red Pierrot feed inside the fleshy leaves of Kalanchoe. Caterpillars of the Milkweed butterflies have bright colours that warn predators of 'distasteful' consequences.

Swallowtail caterpillars look like fresh bird-droppings in their first four instars. After the third moult, they are leaf-green with a false eye-spot on each side, which gives them a snake-like appearance. If all these protective adaptations fail, the Swallowtail caterpillar curls back towards the tormentor and from behind its head comes out a bright orange, forked organ, called the 'osmaterium', that emits a strong odour. Some caterpillars drop down on the ground, merge with the leaf litter, and crawl back on the food plant after the danger has passed.

The caterpillars of some Lycaenids have evolved a very effective strategy to protect themselves. They possess a 'honey gland' on the abdomen, which secretes a sweet liquid attractive to ants. The ants feed on the liquid and, in return, they protect the caterpillar, mainly from wasps. The ants also watch over them when they are pupae and only bid them goodbye when they are ready to fly.

Most pupae are well camoulflaged to look like a leaf or a broken dry twig (for example, the pupae of the Common Mime), so that their detection is almost impossible. On the other hand, the pupa of the Common Crow shines quite conspicuously. Probably, its irradiance serves as a warning to its predators of its distasteful contents. Even in their quiescent stage, some Swallowtail pupae, when disturbed, make snake-like hissing sounds by moving their rear segments.

The period during which the insect remains in the pupal stage depends on the season. If the proper food plant is not available, the pupae go into a hibernation-like stage and emerge as insects only in the next season when the plant is available.

The most vulnerable stage in the adult butterfly's life is immediately after its emergence from the pupa, when its wings are wet and limp. Probably, that is the reason why, most often, butterflies emerge around dawn, when the light is poor—this gives them a better chance of escaping detection. Once on the wing, a butterfly is able to evade many predators. The danger to it then lurks among the flowers and foliage in the form of well-camouflaged spiders, praying mantises, lizards, frogs, and birds. While in flight, it may get ensnared in webs or be preyed upon by dragonflies and robberflies.

Colour plays an important role in the adult butterfly's survival. Most species, which are brightly coloured on the uppersides of their wings, have subdued colours on the undersides, and this camouflages them when at rest. The Blue Oakleaf is a classic example of such coloration. It has on the undersides of its wings the exact colour pattern of a dead leaf, complete with stalk, midrib, and even fungus and worm holes. When disturbed, it opens its wings to take off, flashing its brilliant blue that momentarily startles the predator and gives the butterfly an opportunity to fly away and 'disappear' among the dead leaves, leaving the predator to search for a blue butterfly.

In its DSF, the Common Evening Brown has cryptic, mottled markings on its underside, which enables it to remain undetected while among the dry leaves and stones. In its WSF, this butterfly has a series of eye-spots or ocelli on the undersides, which act as 'target areas' for predators like birds, whose attack is deflected towards the eye-spots instead of some vital part of the butterfly's body. Losing bits of its wing edges does not adversely affect the butterfly. Several of the Lycaenids too have similar adaptations, combining eye-spots with structural features that look like the head with antennae at the rear end. To make this deception convincing, these butterflies often rub their hind wings to create an illusion of a head with actively moving antennae.

MIMICRY

A number of butterflies escape attack because they taste unpleasant. Milkweed butterflies and some Swallowtails store in their adult bodies poisonous fluids consumed by the larvae who eat poisonous plants. The presence of these poisons makes these butterflies unpalatable. Such butterflies are extremely tough and leathery, and this enables them to withstand a trial peck from a bird without seriously injuring the butterfly while the bird learns a lesson. Several of these closely related butterflies resemble each other and that serves to reinforce their 'unpleasant' reputation. Such resemblance is called Mullerian Mimicry.

Some butterflies, however, do not have this in-built protection, but are able to deceive their predators because they resemble some unpalatable species. This form of mimicry is called Batesian Mimicry, in which certain palatable butterflies, to escape predators, have evolved bright and warning colours, and conspicuous patterns, like those of unpalatable species. The mimics not only look like their models, but have the same unhurried flight to advertise their warning colours. This type of mimicry may occur in both sexes as in the Common Mime. This butterfly has two forms: in one form, it mimics the Common Crow and in the other, the Blue Tiger (Plate 8). However, among Eggflies and in the Common Mormon, only the females enjoy this genetic facility of mimicry. The female Great Eggfly mimics the distasteful Common Crow, while the female Danaid Eggfly (Plate 8) is a perfect mimic of the Plain Tiger. The female Common Mormon (Plate 8) is a classic example of Batesian Mimicry. She occurs in three different colour forms. In one (rather uncommon) form, the female looks very much like the male, while in the second and third forms, she mimics two entirely different species of Red-bodied Swallowtails, namely the Crimson Rose and Common Rose. For the success of this type of mimicry, it is essential that the models occur in greater numbers and in the same area, so that the predators encounter more of the real and distasteful models. With every distasteful model attacked, the chances of the mimic's survival increase.

Mimicry is not a conscious effort on the part of creatures, but is a process of selection of favourable genes and elimination of unfit ones. A species might evolve over several generations before the imitation is perfected. Suppose at some point in time a mutant individual is born with a colour closer to that of a distasteful far-off related species, hungry birds feeding on its brothers and sisters may avoid it. So it lives to breed and pass on this protective resemblance until, through a selective process spanning successive generations, the mimics refine themselves to such an extent that they easily pass off for their models. Meanwhile, those individuals who turn out to be poor mimics are more likely to be preyed upon. In this way, butterflies that are not confused for the model are 'corrected', leaving only the perfect copies.

Despite all their protective adaptations, many butterflies, right from the egg stage to the adult stage, do fall prey to birds, lizards, frogs, and other predators. But each protective adaptation is effective in the sense that by rendering these insects less visible, less digestible, or less edible, the attack is, in each case, limited only to a particular type of predator. In the absence of such a process, the destruction would have been total. As butterflies provide food for other creatures, their position in the web of life is vital, and nature has found ways to protect them.

BUTTERFLY MIGRATION

Like birds, some butterflies too migrate. It is indeed amazing that a creature as frail as a butterfly can make arduous and long journeys, but often, the swarms of butterflies during migration are unimaginably large—tens of thousands or even more. Their numbers far surpass even the most massive migrations of birds, mammals, or fish. What is more baffling is that these journeys are usually one-way and the travellers do not return to their place of birth at all. It is the next generation that returns! How then do they find their way back? Several questions relating to insect migration still remain unanswered.

The most exhaustive study of butterfly migration made so far is that of the American Monarch, a Milkweed butterfly that migrates from North America, with its successive breeds reaching as far as Canada to the north in summer, and the progeny returning southwards towards California, Florida, and Mexico, to stay over during winter in communal roosts. In India, two migrations have been observed. In one, at irregular intervals, hundreds and thousands of a particular species or related species of butterflies are seen flying in streams in a definite direction. These are mainly Milkweed butterflies, and Yellows and Whites. Hordes of caterpillars of these butterflies have been noticed stripping all the available food plants bare, to the extent that the successor breed is left without adequate food plants on which to lay eggs. This induces them to move out in search of areas having enough food plants to support the next generation.

The other type of migration takes place regularly, mainly to avoid unfavourable weather conditions and is common among those species that are found in the hills. Such butterflies come down to the plains to avoid extreme cold or heavy rains. The Blue Mormon, for example, is usually found between 2000 and 5000 feet, but in summer, it may ascend up to 7000 feet. However, during the monsoon, it is seen at sea level, flying in

Mumbai's more wooded suburbs where it also breeds. Similarly, in the Himalayas, the Large Cabbage White flies as high as 12,000 feet, but in winter, comes down to breed in the adjoining plains. It is the progeny that return to the Himalayas before the heat becomes oppressive. Strangely enough, some populations of this butterfly do stay as pupae at higher levels in winter, and the adults emerge as the winter withdraws. This is certainly insurance against the migrants failing to return.

The Emigrants, Crimson Rose, Common Crow, and Blue and Common Tigers are some butterflies that migrate quite regularly and are seen roosting together in sheltered plantations or forest patches in extraordinarily large numbers. Such congregations are either prior to their actual migration or during their rest on the way. Butterflies in large numbers have been met mid-sea between India and Sri Lanka, and flocks have been noticed crossing the water along bridges. The world's best known migrant butterfly is the Painted Lady (*Vanessa cardui*) and due to its strong migratory habit, it has spread almost worldwide, as far as the Arctic Circle through Russia. Another international butterfly, which is an accomplished migrant is the diminutive Pea Blue (*Lampides boeticus*). Along the slopes of the Himalayas, it is found in areas as high as 10,000 feet (*c.* 3350 m). It descends to the plains for the winter. Its subsequent progeny return to the high regions as the spring sets in. Neither the Pea Blue nor the Painted Lady have geographical races. This is because their continuous movement prevents the isolation of their population that could give rise to local variations or race creation.

Information on butterfly migration in India is still patchy since it is based purely on observation. The causes of migration have only been guessed at. What is needed is a careful documentation of information on butterfly migration over a prolonged period. Moreover, just as birds are ringed, a butterfly can also be marked with a very tiny label stuck on one of its fore wings, with a serial number and return address. When a butterfly is captured, its details can be recorded, and it can then be released with the label attached. This way, several hundreds of butterflies could be labelled. Of these, only a few may be recaptured or found dead, and sent to the address mentioned. As more and more labelled butterflies are thus recovered, a pattern may emerge of their possible route during migration. Information given by butterfly watchers, of course, will continue to be a valuable contribution that will reinforce scientific findings. This will ultimately help is solving the riddle of butterfly migration.

'BUTTERFLYING'

HOW AND WHERE TO WATCH BUTTERFLIES

Butterfly watching, like bird watching, is an absorbing pursuit. The best part is that butterflies are more easily approached than and as commonly found as birds. All it requires is patience and the art of stalking. But unlike birds, butterflies are late risers. It is only for an hour or so following sunrise that butterflies are seen basking to absorb warmth, feeding on flowers, or chasing each other. That is the time to watch and photograph them. If the temperature is slightly cooler, they are easily approached. However, by midday most of them retreat into the shade, especially along stream banks and in dense foliage.

Butterflies like the Blue, Yellow, and Peacock Pansies, Common Leopard, Tawny Coster, Castors, Common Nawab, Tawny Rajah, Grass Yellow, and Lime are all sun-lovers and enjoy a gambol in open meadows. Milkweed butterflies, Eggflies, Emigrants, Sailors, the Grey, Chocolate, and Lemon Pansies, Barons, Common Mormons, and the Common and Crimson Rose, however, prefer the woodland's edge. Many Browns, like the Tree Brown and Brushbrown, and most Swallowtails, are forest-dwellers. The Browns prefer to stay amongst the undergrowth, while the Swallowtails always seem to be in a great hurry as they flit around tirelessly, pausing only occasionally to hover over a flower or two. The gaudy Jezebel is a common sight even in the middle of a busy city road and in city gardens, it occasionally descends to feed on flowers or hovers around a mango tree, searching for the parasite plant, Mistletoe, on which to lay its eggs. The Evening Brown, with its drab colour, remains hidden among the undergrowth and fallen leaves till dusk, when it comes out, often in large numbers, to flutter around lights. Each species has its favourite flying time and only their general habits are given in this book.

The best time of the year for butterfly watching is just after the rains, till early November. A lesser season is around March and April.

GARDENING FOR BUTTERFLIES

Surprisingly, lilies, gladioli, roses, dahlias, chrysanthemums, and begonias fail to attract butterflies. Instead, these insects would rather settle on a yellow lantana or a pink cockscomb growing wild along the road. They generally prefer purple, yellow, and pink flowers. Among wild flowers, the hardy lantana is the best for attracting butterflies. Its tiny bunched flowers are all-time favourites of these insects. With the right type of plants grown in the garden or even in pots on the balcony or window sill, attracting butterflies is not difficult. Marigold, cosmos, periwinkle (*Vinca rosea*), Mexican sunflower (*Tithonia sp.*), and Verbena, which can all be grown from seeds, are great favourites. Just as butterflies in the northern hills are partial to flowers of Horse Chestnut and Buddleia, Nirgudi (*Vitex negundo*) flowers are most visited by butterflies in the plains. Milkweed butterflies seem to have an affinity for Poinsettia nectar.

Planting food plants for butterflies to lay eggs on is also an interesting way of gardening for butterflies. A lemon plant or curry-leaf plant will bring the Common Mormon and Lime butterfly to lay eggs. Saplings of *amaltas* or Indian laburnum and other Cassias planted in pots will invariably attract the Common Emigrant to lay eggs. The fast-flying Tailed Jay prefers to lay eggs on *sitaphal* or custard apple trees or on false Ashok or mast trees (*Polyalthia sp.*). Ginger lilies (*Hedychium sp.*) will have caterpillars of the Grass Demon Skipper in the rolled up leaves. The pretty little Red Pierrot will have its caterpillars leaf-mining through the fleshy Kalanchoe and Bryophyllum leaves, and Purslane or Office-time (*Portulaca sp.*) will bring both the Eggflies to lay eggs. The Common Crow has a long list of plants on which it lays eggs, and Oleander (*Nerium sp.*), Banyan, Peepal, and other related figs are its favoured food plants. With these few plants around the house, one can watch butterflies from one's doorstep.

Besides nectar, several butterflies, especially the Nymphalids, are readily attracted to fruits like banana, pineapple, or guava, which may be used as baits. However, a Common Nawab or Tawny Rajah is enticed neither by flowers nor by fruits. It takes a rotting crab or prawn to draw them out.

The lives of butterflies seem simple to a passive bystander, but as one peeps into the lifestyle of these colourful insects, fascination to know more about them grows, and then the chase is endless.

REARING CATERPILLARS

Not all insects go through as dramatic a metamorphosis as a butterfly does. The best way to observe this miracle of nature is to rear caterpillars at home and to watch them grow, pupate, and emerge as butterflies.

For beginners, it is better to start off with one of the more common butterflies like the Common Mormon or Common Emigrant, as their caterpillars are quite easy to rear. Caterpillars can be reared in jam jars or plastic bread boxes. The simplest method is to place the caterpillar, along with a spray of loose leaves of its food plant, inside a transparent glass turned upside down. Let this glass stand on a surface of cardboard slightly larger than its diameter. You may also use a jar with a piece of thin cloth or netting over the top instead of the lid. Keep it in a well-lighted spot, but NOT in direct sunlight. Caterpillars require very little air to breathe and will survive even in closed jars for some time. However, air-tight conditions may cause condensation and this encourages fungus. At the same time, excessive dryness can seriously affect the caterpillar's development, especially during moulting, and can cause the food plant to shrivel up.

Food plants must always be fresh, clean, and free of other insects. Stale or wet plants can cause loss of caterpillars due to infection. Food should be changed daily or twice a day and the droppings removed. The absorbent cardboard should be replaced and condensation, if any, should be wiped dry. Avoid overcrowding—the fewer the caterpillars, the better are the chances of successful rearing. While putting in fresh food plants, try to get the caterpillars to wander on to these. They could be persuaded to move with soft brush, but should never be handled or lifted with the fingers as they are easily injured. A caterpillar that is slightly hunched up and that refuses to move may be in the middle of moulting and, therefore, should not be disturbed at all. To watch a plump, hungry caterpillar devouring and demolishing a leaf can be a fascinating pastime, surely no less interesting than watching a goldfish in a bowl!

The caterpillar's growth can be noticed from day to day and when fully grown, it stops eating and becomes restless. It begins to wander, searching for a suitable place to pupate. Usually, twigs kept inside the glass or jar in a slanting position may be chosen for pupation, but caterpillars may also pupate on the side of the jar or its lid. Care should be taken to see that the jar is wide enough for the butterfly to be able to dry its wings after emerging, for if the wet wings get obstructed, the butterfly will be permanently deformed. To avoid this, caterpillars should be reared in fairly large containers. Caterpillars nearing pupation could also be released on potted plants, but then a watch must be kept for straying caterpillars. Once the caterpillar settles to pupate, it must not be pulled off or disturbed. After a day or two, the final shedding takes place to form the pupa. The pupa does not require any care, but in very hot weather, a light spray of water is necessary, especially when the butterfly is about to emerge. As the pupa begins to darken, provide enough twigs around it for the butterfly to climb and crawl on. An hour after it emerges, the butterfly's wings will have hardened enough. Now carry the container outdoors and enjoy the gratifying and exhilarating experience of watching the lovely creature flutter away.

PHOTOGRAPHING BUTTERFLIES

Capturing butterflies on film can be a fascinating experience and is certainly the best way to appreciate the unparalleled beauty of these winged jewels.

Besides getting pretty pictures, the camera's potential to enhance a study is well-recognized. A lot of information can be recorded on film about the butterfly's early stages, habits, and preferred habitats. Most butterflies are shy and will flee at the slightest sign of intrusion into their realm. That makes them some of the most uncooperative and elusive subjects. However, with patience and determination, if one chases them enough with a camera, it is not impossible to get good butterfly pictures.

The first step is to have the proper equipment. Today, most nature photographers work with a 35 mm single lens reflex (SLR) camera, which is quite compact and versatile. Smaller cameras lack the necessary sophistication and are suited only to party and picnic photography, while the large format cameras, besides being expensive, are too cumbersome for most situations. The choice of a camera finally depends on cost and personal preferences. However, even moderately-priced SLR cameras are capable of giving very good results.

Close-up photography does not require a wide assortment of equipment. Ideally, for butterfly photography, a 100 mm macro lens is most suitable. This lens is specially designed to give high quality, close-up images. At the same time, its minimum focusing distance is not too small (as that of the 50 mm macro lens would be), thus giving enough working distance between the photographer and the shy subject and allowing for the use of a flash too. Macro lenses come in different specifications: 50 mm, 60 mm, 90 mm, 100 mm, 105 mm, and even 200 mm. The term 'macro' is often misunderstood. A true macro is a lens capable of 1:1 or greater reproduction at the closest focusing distance. However, 1:2 reproduction is also possible, as some macro lenses are capable of giving only a 1:2 image. To get a life-size (1:1) image, a life-size adaptor is attached between the camera body and lens. The ratio 1:2 means that the image on the film is half as large as the object (or the object is twice as large as the image on the film).

Macro lenses are expensive and are quite scarce in India. Several nature photographers here, therefore, resort to cheaper alternatives, though the results may not be as good as those of a true macro lens. A 50 mm standard lens with a 2 x macro focusing teleconverter attached to the camera body can become a 'macro' lens. Some photographers use a 135 mm or 200 mm tele-lens, with an extension tube (a hollow tube with necessary links between the lens and camera body) attached. This contraption gives a magnification ratio of 1:3, 1:4, 1:5, or even greater. However, 1:5 is the limit and should be used only for larger butterflies like the Swallowtails. Any lens having a greater ratio is just a close focusing lens and not a macro. Supplementary close-up lenses that come in +1, +2, and +3 grades can be screwed on to the front of the standard lens for macro photography. This arrangement works well with flowers, but not with butterflies, as the working distance between the lens and the subject becomes much lesser.

One fact in close-up photography is that, the greater the magnification, the more one loses in terms of light and depth of field. Therefore, photographing in available light, which is often not enough, requires wide aperture with reasonably fast shutter speed to avoid camera shakes. Wide aperture means limited depth of field and this results in the subject being only partly in focus. This problem can be countered by careful focusing and by keeping most of the subject parallel to the film plane as far as possible. A lot is learnt by trial and error, and with frequent practice. Available light can be used creatively to transform an ordinary scene into a great photograph. Overcast conditions provide pleasantly soft and even light that makes the colours come out more vividly on the film. In direct light, a white paper card or a metal foil can be used for reflecting light into dark shadows. However, on several occasions the available natural light is quite poor, especially under a forest canopy or heavily overcast sky, which makes hand-held photography almost impossible. In such situations, the use of an electronic flash becomes necessary.

In macro-photography, a flash is thus an indispensable tool. The flash helps in getting sharp and brilliant pictures in most conditions, and its rapid burst of light eliminates camera shakes and freezes to some extent, the movement of the subject. It is most useful when the available light is not sufficient to permit the use of small apertures like f 16 or f 22 to achieve maximum depth of field. The dark background created by the use of a flash, though often disliked, in fact, gives the appearance of sharpness because of a well-defined edge. The dark background can be reduced by the use of an additional 'fill in' flash that is aimed at the background. However, in the field, it is not always practical to use an additional flash.

To start with, a compact but not too small unit of flash that can be mounted on the camera is good enough. Ideally, the flash should be dedicated to the model of the camera. A dedicated flash system works together with the camera's 'through the lens' (TTL) metering, which measures the amount of light reflected from the subject, or in some systems, from the film's surface, and which cuts off the flash output to give correct exposure with the selected aperture. Such a system is more convenient and saves calculating the flash to subject distance for proper aperture.

As for the film, a good quality film with a speed of 100 ASA is most suitable. Whether to use a slide film or print film depends on the purpose of photography, besides personal preference. Slides or transparencies are used for audio-visuals and are preferred for commercial printing like on calendars and greeting cards. A slide film allows very little margin for error. Any mistake of under or over-exposure will be seen. Thus with slides, it is easy to judge the performance of the photographer as well as of the camera. On the other hand, print film does provide some margin for over and under-exposure errors and, further, such errors can be corrected while making prints from the negative.

One can have the best equipment, but these gadgets will not get great pictures if the photographer lacks patience and initiative to go out and try again and again. Stalking butterflies in the field can be very frustrating at times. One has to develop chameleon-like habits. Bright coloured clothes should be avoided. Dull shades of grey and green provide good camouflage. Never let your shadow fall over or near the butterfly. Approach as close as you can to get an image that will show details. Always pre-set all camera controls and then creep slowly towards the butterfly until it is in focus. You will have to develop a slow, gentle gait, as any sudden movement will scare the subject away.

The best time to photograph butterflies is in the morning, between 7.30 and 9.30 a.m. After this, they get 'charged' by the heat of the sun and are generally very wary. Cool mornings are real blessings, for they bring butterflies to bask in the sun and these will not readily fly until their bodies are warm enough, thus providing a marvellous opportunity to get photographs at close quarters. Hot days will bring thirsty butterflies to damp patches near streams, rivers, and water falls. Of course, waiting near preferred flowers like lantana, cockscomb, or eupatorium can give lovely pictures. Butterflies that do not come to flowers could be baited with beer, toddy, fermented jaggery, or overripe fruits. Planting butterfly food plants will provide opportunities to photograph butterfly life-cycles. Just getting pretty pictures should not be the only aim—it is also worth photographing butterflies while courting, mating, laying eggs, emerging from the pupa, feeding, or even while being eaten. This gives dimensions to the theme and proves the photographer's skill and enterprise. Good butterfly pictures need investment in time and film, patience and perseverance, and a dedicated and adventurous photographer will definitely get rewarding results.

Here are some useful tips on how to photograph butterflies:

1. Compose the frame carefully, filling it with what is essential and eliminating what distracts. Include the background only if it enhances the composition. Before clicking, check the edges and corners of the frame to ensure everything that is wanted is included.
2. Try out different angles and check for battered or bird-pecked wings before photographing, for they do not make commercially pretty pictures. (On the other hand, you may just be looking out for such survivors.)
3. Always duplicate promising shots with slight under-exposure and then slight over-exposure to get properly exposed pictures. Under-exposure deepens colours and darkens the background, while over-exposure produces a pastel effect.
4. In close-ups, everything cannot be sharp, therefore focus carefully with purpose and be sure that essential regions like the head are perfectly sharp. Use the highest f-stops (smallest apertures) possible and add light with the reflector or flash.
5. Develop patience to cope with changes of light and your subject's willingness to 'pose'. Be prepared to stalk the butterfly over a long distance until it finally settles. Get down on the ground, wade into water, or crawl through bushes, but learn to remain motionless when the situation demands it.

BUTTERFLIES AND CONSERVATION

Today, all over the world, mere sustenance cannot be the only concern of human beings. The need to produce food, fibre, and wood is much greater than ever before. This has led to large tracts of forests being clear-felled and other natural areas giving way to urbanization, pollution, overgrazing, or intensive agriculture. Loss of prime habitat is the major threat to all wildlife, including butterflies. The exact status of several species of Indian butterflies is still not clearly known. To initiate a conservation programme for these insects, one needs, first of all, a detailed study of their life histories and the factors governing their survival.

Among Indian butterflies, the Kaiser-i-Hind that is found in the Himalayan forests is the rarest and is listed in the *Red Data Book: Threatened Swallowtail Butterflies of the World.* The Bhutan Glory, too, is listed as a rare species in the *Red Data Book*, along with some Apollos that fly in the Himalayas. Most Indian butterflies are now protected by law, that is, under the Wildlife Protection Act, 1972, which says that catching and killing of certain species is illegal unless permitted under a licence. However, laws on paper are not likely to save wildlife unless enough measures are taken simultaneously to protect their habitats and to generate public awareness of their role and utility in maintaining the ecological balance.

What started as a hobby in the sixteenth and seventeenth centuries, catching butterflies for trade is big business today, with a world turnover of between US $ 20 to 30 million per year. Several thousands of dead butterflies are supplied to scientists, museums, and private collections, and to producers of fancy items for the general market. Surprisingly, it has been found that butterfly populations can be harvested in a sustainable way, provided the habitat is good enough. The butterfly industry that has developed in Papua New Guinea has shown that trade and conservation can be mutually beneficial in providing local employment and easing the pressure on the wild population, while still enriching the habitat. Farming of certain endangered species of butterflies can also be used as a conservation measure to restock their depleted population.

Butterflies are found in a variety of habitats, from traffic island gardens in the middle of busy roads to verdant forests. Like other insects, they have an important place in the web of life and being closely associated with plant life, they are the first to be affected by even the slightest disturbance to their habitat. Several of these splendid insects are exclusive forest dwellers and, being conspicuous, their presence or absence serves to monitor ecological changes in habitat, thus warning us about the deteriorating environment.

GLOSSARY

abdomen: the last of the three major body divisions of an insect larva, pupa, or adult; it contains the digestive and reproductive organs

aedeagus: the penis; the male intromittent organ

androconia: the long scent scales on a male butterfly

antennae: the pair of long-stalked, jointed sensory organs coming forward from the head, with an enlarged club at or near the tip in butterflies

anterior: towards the head

apex: the tip of the fore wing

Batesian Mimicry: the acquired resemblance of an edible butterfly species (the mimic) to a distasteful or poisonous butterfly species (the model) for protection from predators

Binomial (system): the system of naming animals and plants by their genus and species names (Latin)

cell: a space in the centre of a wing enclosed by veins

chitin: horny material composing much of the external skeleton of an insect

chrysalis: butterfly pupa

claws: terminal hooks at the end of the tarsus (foot)

compound eye: a group of hundreds of small eye units called ommatidia, each with its own lens and sensory cells

courtship: the behavioral sequence of male and female actions prior to copulation or mating

coxa: basal segment of a leg, next to the body

cremaster: an organ of attachment of the pupa to its support, formed from the anal plate area of the last abdominal segment of the larva and often involving tiny hooks or spines to catch in the silk pupation pad

crochets: hooks on the ends of the prolegs of caterpillars

diapause: a resting state, such as estivation (over summer or a hot, dry period) and hibernation (over winter or a cold period)

dimorphism: occurrence in two forms
dorsal: relating to the upper surface
exoskeleton: skeleton covering the outside of the body, or situated in the skin
facet: a single, six-sided unit in the butterfly's compound eye
family: a group used in classification, consisting of a number of related genera, tribes, or subfamilies; similar families are grouped in an order
femur: the third segment of an insect leg, often the longest; it is sturdy and undivided
food plant: the host plant on which the larva of a butterfly feeds
frenulum: a long, strong bristle or bunch of bristles at the base of the leading margin of the hind wing of most moths. It locks onto the fore wing and holds the wings together
genitalia: the external reproductive organs
genus (pl. genera): a group used in classification, consisting of a number of related species or subgenera; similar genera are grouped in a family
geographic races and subspecies: groups of geographically-separated populations of the same species with somewhat different patterns, colours, sizes, or other physical evidence of adaptive responses to differing environmental conditions
girdle: a silken thread spun around the thorax area of the larva and attached to an adjoining twig, the same twig, or any other surface
hair pencil: a group of long, hair-like scales found at the end of the abdomen of male butterflies; these are scent distributors
head: the first of three major divisions of the insect body, bearing the eyes, antennae, and mouth parts
Himalaya: the entire mountain range from Kashmir in the west to Arunachal Pradesh in the east
instar: the period between two larval moults
larva (in butterflies): caterpillar
lateral: on the sides
metamorphosis: the series of developmental stages through which a butterfly passes; from the egg to larva to pupa to adult
micropyle: an opening in the top of an egg through which the sperm passes to fertilize the egg
migration: periodic movement of individuals or groups between two geographic regions
mimicry: the resemblance of one individual to another or to a natural object; usually an aid to survival
moulting: shedding the exoskeleton during growth

mudpuddling: seeking moisture (besides dissolved salts) from damp soil; mainly to flush out body wastes
Mullerian Mimicry: the acquired resemblance of several distasteful butterfly species to each other, all being avoided by predators
nomenclature: scientific names applied in a classification system
Northeastern India: region including Assam, Meghlaya, Nagaland, Manipur, Mizoram, Tripura, and Arunachal Pradesh
ocellus: a coloured spot (often with a white or black 'pupil') surrounded by a ring of another colour
ommatidia: the thousands of hexagonal eye units grouped in the compound eyes of a butterfly
osmaterium: a Y-shaped, fleshy organ that can be protruded from the top of the prothorax in Swallowtail larvae, and which produces a strong odour
palp or palpus: a three-segmented sensory organ (often hairy in appearance) projecting in front of the head
peninsular India: region south of the Tapti river
posterior: to the rear
proboscis: the sucking tube coiled under the adult butterfly's head and used for drinking fluids
pupa (in butterflies): the chrysalis; an inactive, mummy-like stage with appendages tightly enclosed. In this stages, the larval structures are drastically reorganized into those of the adult
scales: highly-modified, flattened hairs that form a roof tile-like covering on the membranous wings
scent tuft: a tuft of scent hairs displayed by some male Hesperids, Nymphalids, and other butterflies during courtship segment: a ring-like or tubular division of the body or of an appendage like a leg or antenna that is bounded by sutures
sex patch or brand: a patch of androconia on the male
sexual dimorphism: a striking difference in colour and form between the males and females of a species
silk gland: a gland that passes silk threads out through a spinneret
simple eye: a single eye on the head of a caterpillar; this composed of a lens and sensory units
species: the smallest unit of classification commonly used, consisting of a number of related organisms or populations capable of inter-breeding similar species that are grouped in a genus
sphragus: a hard, horny structure secreted by the male Apollo on to the abdomen of the female during copulation; it prevents the female from mating with other males

spinneret: an internal tube ending in a pore from which issues a viscous fluid that hardens into a silky fibre; used in spinning larval pads for pupation or in dropping from a leaf

spiracles: respiratory openings on the sides of insect larvae, pupae, and adults

subfamily: a group of related genera or tribes within a family

superfamily: a group of related families; there are two superfamilies of butterflies, the Hesperoidea (Skippers) and the Papilionoidea (true butterflies).

tail: a slender, scale-covered, membranous projection from the posterior lateral edge of the hind wing, found in certain Swallowtails, Lycaenids, Pierids, Nymphalids, and Hesperiids.

tarsus: the fifth division or foot part of the leg; it usually consists of five subdivisions and a terminal pair of claws

thorax: the second of the three major divisions of the insect body, bearing the six legs and four wings

tibia: fourth segment of a leg, between the femur and tarsus; it is usually long and slender, and is undivided

trachea: a thin-walled respiratory tube in insects

tribe: a group of related genera or subtribes

tubercle: a small projection on the skin of a caterpillar or the surface of an egg; often with spines

ventral: lower surface

Western Ghats: for our purposes, this includes the entire range of the Sahyadris, north to south, including the Nilgiris, Palni, Annamalai, and associated hills in Karnataka, Tamil Nadu, and Kerala

INDEX

INDEX